mattachine
REVIEW
REVOLT OF THE
HOMOSEXUAL
ACT UP
COME OUT
T0054447
0 1 2 3 4 5 6
one
IT'S GAY O'CLOCK!
I'M COMING OUT
Christopher St
ACT UP

Christopher St
mattachine
REVIEW
REVOLT OF THE
HOMOSE XUAL
ACT UP
COME
OUT
HATE FREE
HUMAN
I
Know
You
Know
0 1 2 3 4 5 6
IT'S GAY
O'CLOCK!
one
I'M

The Gay Agenda

A Modern Queer History & Handbook

Ashley Molesso + Chess Needham

MORROW GIFT

An Imprint of William Morrow

For information, address HarperCollins Publishers,
195 Broadway, New York, NY 10007.

HarperCollins books may be purchased for educational, business, or sales promotional use. For information, please email the Special Markets Department at SPsales@harpercollins.com.

FIRST EDITION

DESIGNED BY KYLE O'BRIEN

Library of Congress Cataloging-in-Publication Data has been applied for.

ISBN 978-0-06-294455-9

22 23 24 IM 10 9 8 7 6 5 4 3 2

this book is for

all of the people in this world who have ever felt "different" from society's standards, who have ever questioned who they are, who have ever felt like they needed to be someone they weren't out of fear, and for the people who have the strength to live out in the open, like the big queer role models they are.

CONTENTS

a few Gay Notes from the authors

Introduction

When we were approached by our super cool agent via Instagram (LOL! How very 2018), she asked us if we wanted to write an illustrated book about anything. Literally anything in the world! We came up with a bunch of crazy ideas—fashion throughout the decades as modeled by dogs, a children's book about a dog who can't bark, and so on. But we landed on this—*The Gay Agenda*. It was actually a revelation, as we found out that a pastor from a church in Arkansas that Ash previously attended wrote a book of the same title. It had a slightly . . . different theme. So this book was meant to be.

We were excited to be able to use our voices to share some of the history of and information about our ever-changing and ever-growing community. The first section is history. And hopefully not boring history. But it wasn't until we started our research that we realized how little we knew about the past of our very own community. Learning about our history made us feel stupid at times—how could we call ourselves part of the queer community and yet know so little about those who paved the way for us to live out and proud? As we researched, we discovered so much about how modern gay history is woven into the threads of "regular" history—that is, the history you read about in textbooks—but, because it is rarely highlighted, it remains unknown. While writing the book, we've become familiar with historical events and figures that were new to us and learned about the enormity of the struggle of the gay liberation movement.

As you read the history section of this book, we would like you to keep in mind that not every fact, event, and figure is covered. That isn't to diminish the impact of them, but merely because we had to be selective. We tried to

GAY IS GOOD

be representational. We know that history is often whitewashed, and therefore there are likely hundreds of people who made a huge impact on our community whose names were never documented anywhere, and therefore continue to not be documented here, but we honor them anyway.

We call this a gay history book, but we also hope that in due time, gay history will just be history, and these events will be seen as a part of the bigger picture, which is our past, present, and future.

The second section of the book is informational. For us, getting to know ourselves and our identities has been an ever-changing process. Growing up queer, even today, is hard. We hope that if someone who is questioning themselves or their identity reads this, they can begin to better understand themselves or feel empowered to get to know themselves. We hope that if someone who feels alone gets to read this, they know that they are among a community of many. We hope that if someone who has a queer child and doesn't understand them gets their hands on this, they begin to understand that their child is part of a community and not an anomaly. We just hope that our little labor of love brings something to you.

If you or someone you know is in crisis or in need of a safe space to talk, call one of the LGBTQ+-friendly resources below:

Trevor Lifeline — 1-866-488-7386
Crisis Text Line — Text HOME to 741741
National Runaway Safeline — 1-800-RUNAWAY
Trans Lifeline — 1-877-565-8860

PRE-1900s

Not surprisingly, gay stuff has been going on forever. As far back as **9600** B.C.E., art depicts male pairings that could be interpreted as homosexual intercourse. Some Bronze Age drawings even show figures with breasts and male genitalia. As sources from before the **1900s** are largely anecdotal, this book focuses more on the twentieth century and beyond. Here's a sampling of some interesting events and people from this earlier era to give a quick summary before getting into the context of the modern queer liberation movement.

~600 B.C.E.

Sappho, a Greek lyric poet, was born on the island of Lesbos. Though much of her poetry has been lost, and little is known of her life, she is revered as an icon of love and desire between women, hence the words "sapphic" and "lesbian" being used to describe women who love women (WLW). It is uncertain if Sappho really was a lesbian (meaning woman who loves women . . . not someone from Lesbos. She definitely was from Lesbos), as some also characterized her as a promiscuous heterosexual—however, there is Hellenistic testimony that discusses Sappho's lesbianism. While her sexuality is still debated, it is generally accepted that her poetry, at least, celebrated homoerotic feelings between women.

The Book of Leviticus

~538–330 B.C.E.

Okay, this is a big one. Like, a really big one. The Book of Leviticus states both "A man shall not lie with a male as with a woman; it is an abomination"; and "If a man lies with a male as with a woman, both of them have committed an abomination; they shall be put to death; their blood is upon them." The repercussions of these verses have been huge: they've caused people to be kicked out of families, churches, communities, and so on. These passages are often cited as a way to negate homosexuality on the basis of religion. Which sucks. Because the Bible is just a historical document and should be read with the understanding of the historical time it was written in. The Bible also says, "An eye for an eye, a tooth for a tooth," and people seem to be able to interpret that part . . .

THE WARREN CUP

~5–15 C.E.

The Warren Cup is an ancient silver cup that is beautifully decorated in relief images of men having sex with other men! In ancient Rome, there was a ton of homoerotic art, although it is less common than depictions of heterosexual eroticism. The cup is named after Edward Perry Warren, an American art collector.

There's about to be a big break in history. But it's not because nothing happened for us homos, it's just because a lot of it is repetitive. Like, more gay art was found. More countries said being gay is bad. Some decriminalized homosexuality (don't get excited, this doesn't mean that homosexuals were treated well, just that being a homo was no longer an explicitly illegal act). Some countries executed homosexuals. A gay bar was opened in Japan (okay, that one is pretty cool, but there's not a lot of information about it).

KARL HEINRICH ULRICHS

AUGUST 28, 1825–JULY 14, 1895

Karl Heinrich Ulrichs, a German lawyer and author, was an extremely early gay pioneer. He came out to friends and family as "Urning," or a third gender that typically describes a female psyche in a man's body, and began to write about homosexual love. He claimed it was natural. His first pieces of writing were under a pseudonym, but shortly after publishing, he came out and began to write under his real name. In 1867, Ulrichs became the first person to speak publicly in defense of homosexuality (despite the term not being used yet), begging for a resolution to repeal anti-homosexual German laws. Ulrichs would often run into trouble with the law due to his controversial writing, and many of his books were banned and confiscated. Ulrichs is now a cult figure—there is an annual street party and poetry reading at the Karl-Heinrich-Ulrichs-Platz in Munich to celebrate his birthday.

THE TWO-SPIRIT FROM ZUNI!

1849–1896

Some members of the Zuni tribe were once described by their community as *lhamana*, which is now known as Two-Spirit, or a third gender. We'wha, one of the most famous Two-Spirit people, was a Zuni Native American from New Mexico. Although they were born biologically male, they trained in traditional "feminine" roles, like cooking, crafting, and offering spiritual guidance. As white people began to usurp land from Native Americans, Protestant missionaries began to infiltrate their tribe—the Grant administration aimed to assimilate Native Americans into U.S. society by converting them to Christianity rather than move them onto reservations. They were not very successful, though We'wha did learn some more crafts from the white family they worked for. We'wha became close to many settlers and was interested in learning English. They ended up making crafts for many, and their pottery was later displayed at the National Museum in Washington, D.C. Because they learned English, We'wha became the de facto representative for their tribe and was the first of the tribe to travel to Washington, D.C. We'wha died at the age of forty-seven from heart failure.

OSCAR WILDE

OCTOBER 16, 1854–NOVEMBER 30, 1900

Oscar Wilde, an Irish poet and playwright, was one of the most beloved playwrights of the late nineteenth century, and is also well known for his criminal conviction for homosexuality. Wilde was a well-known poet and produced several society comedies, including *The Importance of Being Earnest* and *Lady Windermere's Fan*. At the peak of Wilde's fame, the marquess of Queensberry, a Scottish nobleman who was the father of Wilde's lover, left a note at Wilde's club publicly accusing Wilde of sodomy. Wilde brought libel charges against the marquess, but the marquess avoided prison by proving his accusation true. Lawyers investigated Wilde and found that he was indeed a homosexual, and the tables turned. Now, instead of the marquess being convicted, Wilde was forced to try to prove that he was not a homosexual. He lost the case and had to pay all the legal expenses, which left him bankrupt. Convicted of sodomy and gross indecency, Wilde was advised to flee the country to France. Instead, he stayed and served a two-year sentence at hard labor. Wilde was released in 1897 and moved to France. Due to the harsh conditions in prison, he was in poor health. He continued to write, but he fell into alcoholism, developed meningitis, and died on November 30, 1900.

1900s -1940s

EMMA GOLDMAN MAGNUS HIRSCHFELD THE SOCIETY FOR HUMAN RIGHTS VICE VERSA RADCLYFFE HALL PANSY CRAZE THE PINK TRIANGLE THE KINSEY SCALE

JUNE 27, 1869–MAY 14, 1940

Emma Goldman was way, *waaay* ahead of her time. She spent her life as an anarchist, political activist, writer, and outspoken leader on women's rights and social issues. Her speeches on women's rights attracted thousands (which was a big deal back then!), often advocating the use of contraception and encouraging "free love" (which was also a big deal back then!). As first-wave feminism and suffragists had brought the issue of women's rights to light, Goldman's advocacy for women was not unprecedented; however, her stance on prejudice against homosexuals was virtually unheard of. She argued that social liberation should extend to homosexuals—she was the first public figure to defend homosexuality to the general public, and often did so during speaking tours. That's pretty cool!

"to the daring belongs the future."

Magnus Hirschfeld

MAY 14, 1868–MAY 14, 1935

Magnus Hirschfeld, a German sexologist and friend of Emma Goldman's, founded the Institute for Sex Research in Germany, which housed a library on sexuality and provided educational services and consultations. People from all over Europe flocked to the institute to learn about their sexuality—it was one of the first establishments to study this taboo topic! Hirschfeld often used the term "transvestite" in his work to describe what we now know as transgender people. He was revolutionary in that he not only provided research and education, but also opened the doors of the institute to "transvestites," offering them room and board, shelter, gender-corrective surgeries, and jobs. Unfortunately, when the Nazis took power in 1933, the institute was ransacked, thousands of books and research papers were burned, staff and boarders were beaten, and ultimately the institute was forced to close its doors forever. Hirschfeld and his lover sought sanctuary in France, where he died in 1935.

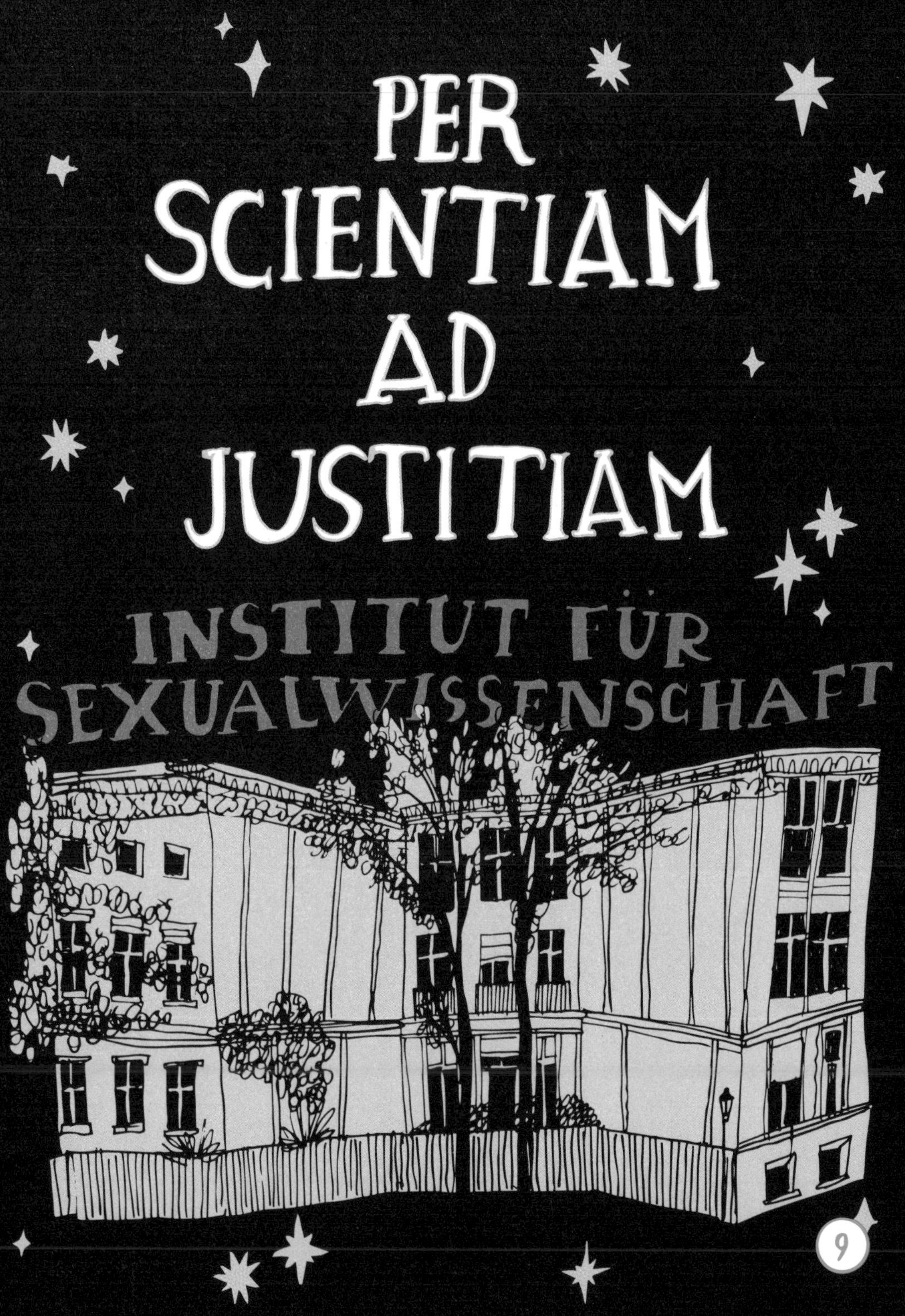
PER SCIENTIAM AD JUSTITIAM
INSTITUT FÜR SEXUALWISSENSCHAFT

The Society for Human Rights

1924

The Society for Human Rights, the first known homosexual organization in the United States, was established by Henry Gerber in Chicago in 1924, on the coattails of Magnus Hirschfeld's work. Gerber himself was a gay German immigrant who had settled in Chicago but was temporarily sent to a mental institution in 1917 due to his homosexuality. Following his release from the institution, Gerber enlisted in the army and was stationed in Germany, where he learned about Hirschfeld's work and the gay scene in Berlin. He decided, upon return to the United States, to try to organize. He applied for

HENRY GERBER HOUSE

a charter from the state of Illinois to start a nonprofit organization to protect the interests of "people who by reasons of mental and physical abnormalities are abused and hindered in the legal pursuit of happiness which is guaranteed them by the Declaration of Independence," and subsequently produced the very first American publication geared toward homosexuals—*Friendship and Freedom* However, very few of the original seven members of the organization actually signed up to receive it, for fear that postal inspectors would deem the publication obscene under the Comstock Laws—a set of laws that criminalized using the U.S. Postal Service to send any "obscene" items such as sex toys, letters with sexual content, contraceptives, or verbal obscenity. Only two issues of *Friendship and Freedom* were produced, and no copies are known to exist today. Gerber sought to expand the membership of the society, but had limited it to only gay men, not women or bisexuals. He could not obtain financial support, and many were reluctant to join. One of the founding members, unbeknownst to the group, had a wife and children (oops) who found out about the group and exposed it to the *Chicago Examiner*. This basically marked the end of the society, as Gerber and other members were arrested (although never charged), and the organization was dismissed as a "strange sex cult" by the press. Despite its short lifespan, the Society for Human Rights was a small step toward LGBTQ+ organization and activism, and Henry Gerber's original Chicago apartment, where he founded the society, was designated a national historic landmark in 2015.

FRIENDSHIP AND FREEDOM

Vice Versa

1947

The very first lesbian publication, ***Vice Versa***, was published by a twenty-five-year-old secretary under the pseudonym "Lisa Ben" (an anagram for "lesbian"—sneaky). Because she worked in an office, Lisa had access to a company typewriter and carbon paper and the ability to make copies. Nine issues of ten copies each were produced. Although the publication was short-lived, it served as a forerunner for other, longer-standing gay American publications.

VICE VERSA

June, 1947 Volume 1, Number Issue 1

TABLE OF CONTENTS

IN EXPLANATION..............1
DRAMA REVIEW..............3
FILM REVIEW..............9
VERSE..............14

Radclyffe Hall

AUGUST 12, 1880–OCTOBER 7, 1943

In 1928, Radclyffe Hall published *The Well of Loneliness*, a lesbian novel, which was highly controversial for portraying homosexuality as natural (though it did not include any overtly sexual references). A British court judged it obscene, but the publicity of the legal battle brought visibility and awareness of homosexuality to British and American cultures. Although there wasn't really much of an understanding of gender and sexuality at this time, Radclyffe considered themselves a "congenital invert"—a term used by sexologists in the nineteenth and early twentieth centuries to describe an "inversion" of gender traits. Regardless of labels, Radclyffe was often photographed wearing dapper, totally badass three-piece suits and would no doubt be Insta-famous today.

PANSY CRAZE!
HAMILTON LODGE
BALL IS SCENE
OF SPLENDOR

the great drag balls of the 1930s

1920s–1930s

Way, way back in the day, people held masquerade balls, because isn't it so fun to dress up as someone else more than just once a year on Halloween? Wearing masks and dressing in drag among strangers was a way for gay men and women to be fabulous (and cross-dress) in secret! Anyway, the gays decided to put their own fantastic and campy twist on these masked balls, and they became a huge hit, attracting even heterosexual attendees, thus beginning early movements of what we know today as drag and camp culture. Deemed the Pansy Craze, this was a moment in time when balls were so popular that they were going on all over the country. Toward the end of Prohibition, speakeasies would openly advertise drag entertainment to their mix of hetero and queer customers because it was so popular. Dressing in drag and partying all night went hand in hand with the Prohibition laws that were in force at the time. And balls like these are still a huge part of drag culture today!

The PiNK T

1930S–1940S

In Nazi concentration camps, each prisoner was made to wear a badge identifying the reason for their imprisonment. Just as the yellow star was used to identify Jews, the pink triangle was used to distinguish those imprisoned for being homosexual, bisexual, or transgender. After the war, some prisoners were lucky enough (that sounds weird: Is it lucky to survive after watching others die?) to be liberated from concentration camps; however, many of the homosexuals liberated from the camps were reincarcerated by the Federal Republic of Germany, which classified homosexuality as a felony until 1969.

1969! In the 1970s, gay liberation activists repurposed the hateful badge into a symbol of gay pride and liberation that is still used today. Most popularly, in 1987, at the height of the AIDS crisis, the symbol was used accompanied by the words "Silence = Death" by the advocacy group ACT UP.

RiANGLE
SILENCE=DEATH

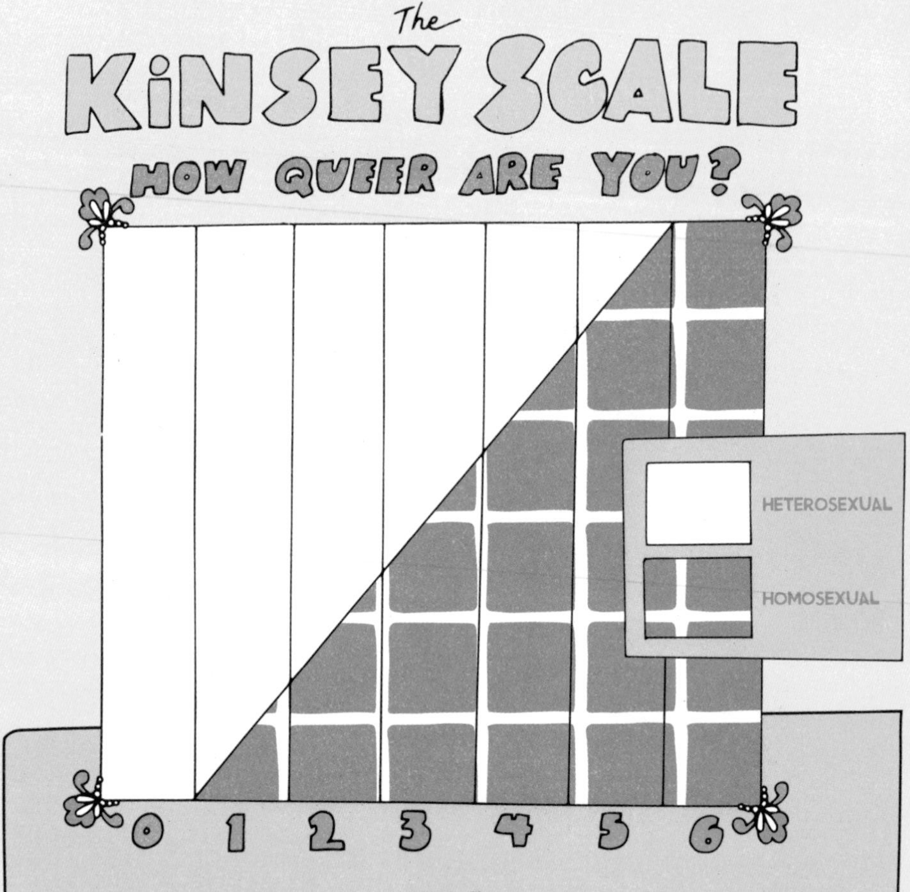

1948

The Kinsey scale was developed by Alfred Kinsey to prove that sexuality is most often confined to one of two distinct categories—homosexual and heterosexual—but rather exists on a continuum and is subject to change over time (this seems obvious now). This was key in defining the fact that homosexuality, in one form or the other, exists in a huge percentage of the population, not a "freakish" and small group—and that due to the heterosexual norm, many people don't ever question their sexuality. The report in which the scale was first published, *Sexual Behavior in the Human Male*, was also notable because most studies prior to this were conducted by medical professionals as a means of attempting to change their subjects' sexual orientation, not to actually gather data and study sexuality. The implications of this scale acknowledged a fluidity in human sexual behavior and began the process of normalizing homosexuality and challenging traditional heteronormative worldviews.

1950s

THE LAVENDER SCARE THE MATTACHINE SOCIETY LESBIAN PULP FICTION HOMOSEXUALITY AS A MENTAL ILLNESS ONE, INC. DAUGHTERS OF BILITIS JAMES BALDWIN FRANK KAMENY COOPER DO-NUTS RIOT

THE LAVENDER SCARE

LATE 1940S–1960S

The Red Scare, a congressional witch hunt searching for members of the Communist Party during the early years of the Cold War, is well known. However, the Lavender Scare, during which thousands of gay employees were either fired or forced to resign from their federal jobs due to their sexuality, is less so. By the end of World War II, many people had moved into urban America and had begun to make their own social communities, leaving rural, insular lives behind. By the late 1940s, the general public was becoming more and more aware of the existence of homosexuality; the Kinsey scale had even proved that homosexual feelings were common. Despite this widespread awakening, homosexuality was still not accepted as natural, because virtually *nobody* was open about their sexuality. Gay men were labeled perverts or sexual psychopaths.

In 1950, Senator Joseph McCarthy, an anti-Communist, began to link Communism and homosexuality. His political rhetoric worked, and the general public developed the impression that homosexuals were morally weak, were psychologically disturbed, and undermined the traditional family (now this really sounds familiar, doesn't it?). He also alleged that homosexuals were more susceptible to blackmail since they had to hide their sexuality. These smear tactics led to a 1953 executive order signed by Dwight D. Eisenhower that barred homosexuals from working in the federal government. Hundreds of gay people were forcibly outed and fired from the State Department, the military, and other branches of the government. This policy stayed in place until Bill Clinton signed a 1995 executive order stating that the U.S. government would not discriminate based on race, color, religion, sex, national origin, disability, or sexual orientation.

The Mattachine Society

1950

One of the earliest LGBTQ+ rights organizations, the Mattachine Society, founded in Los Angeles, California, called for a radical movement of gay people to challenge anti-gay oppression and strive to build a gay community. This was known as the homophile movement. The society sponsored social events, held fund-raisers, and published newsletters. In the mid-1950s, the Mattachine Society turned its efforts toward protesting the police's entrapment of gay men and other oppressive tactics. The group's founders were Communists, and as they became more political, public scrutiny and pressure steadily increased. As McCarthyism grew, a division arose in the society, leading the original founders to resign in 1953. Under new leadership, the group changed its goals, focusing less on social change and gay power, and more on accommodating heterosexuals and being nonconfrontational. Membership dwindled and the society's national structure dissolved by the end of the decade.

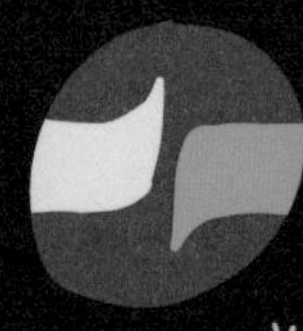

MATTACHINE SOCIETY, INC.

Lesbian Pulp Fiction

1950s

Have you ever come across an old paperback in a used bookstore with some babes on the cover looking suspiciously gay, accompanied by an even more suspiciously gay title, like ***Another Kind of Love*** (Paula Christian) or ***These Curious Pleasures*** (Sloane Britain)? Or maybe you've seen the ones that tell all on the cover, with titles like ***Adam and Two Eves*** (Anonymous) and ***I Prefer Girls*** (Jessie Dumont)? Welcome to the fascinating world of lesbian pulp fiction. This genre of novels became popular in the 1950s and '60s, and many of the authors published under pseudonyms or anonymously. The books often presented the rude underlying moral that lesbians don't get happy endings: the plot formula always featured a forbidden love, most definitely followed by death, disaster, and the like. ***The Price of Salt*** by Claire Morgan was the first exception to this, and many of you may know it by the name of ***Carol***, renamed in the 1990s and republished under the author's true name, Patricia Highsmith. It was also made into a movie by Todd Haynes in 2015! Lesbian pulp's purpose was basically porn before the Internet—quick, sloppy reads aimed at male readers, though many curious women found truth and longing in reading these. And look at that cover art! So classic, so queer.

Homosexuality as a mental illness

1952

In 1952, the American Psychiatric Association published the first edition of the ***Diagnostic and Statistical Manual of Mental Disorders***, also known as the ***DSM-I***, in which homosexuality was described as a "sociopathic personality disturbance." This was not at all controversial at the time and coincided well with societal standards of the 1950s. When the ***DSM-II*** was released in 1968, fourteen years later, homosexuality was reclassified as a sexual deviation. The timing of this release coincided with the gay rights movement, and gay activists would challenge the classification. Homosexuality remained a mental illness until its declassification in 1973.

ONE, INC.

1953–PRESENT

ONE, Inc., was a gay rights organization that produced the long-lasting magazine *One*. *One* magazine contained stories about homosexual love and was heavily scrutinized by the USPS and the FBI, until October 1954, when the postmaster officially declared the magazine "obscene" under the Comstock Laws. The specifically "obscene" issue contained a story called "Sappho Remembered," about a lesbian couple; a poem about cruising; and an advertisement for the magazine *The Circle* (which was also geared toward homosexual romance stories). ONE, Inc, filed lawsuits protesting the obscenity ruling, which went all the way to the U.S. Supreme Court in 1958. The court ruled that writings that describe love affairs between two homosexuals were *not* obscene. This was the first U.S. Supreme Court ruling to deal with the First Amendment's free speech rights as they relate to homosexuality. The magazine ended publication in 1969.

THE LADDER
75¢
The Ladder
a Lesbian Review
The Ladder
The Ladder

Daughters of Bilitis

1955

The Daughters of Bilitis was one of the first lesbian organizations established, essentially the lesbian response to the beginnings of the homophile movement. There were very few ways for gays to meet other gays, since most weren't publicly out, so this organization was like a "secret club" for lesbians. It was initially created as an alternative to lesbian bars, because at this time many gay and lesbian bars were subject to police raids and harassment and were not always the most enjoyable places to link up. As the group's membership grew, its aims shifted to provide support for women who were afraid to come out, educating them on their rights. Formed in San Francisco, the organization had expanded within a year to have members in New York City, Los Angeles, Chicago, and Rhode Island. (All the cool places. And Rhode Island.) As they were unable to advertise in newspapers, founders Del Martin and Phyllis Lyon began a newsletter to distribute among women. This newsletter became *The Ladder*, the first nationally distributed lesbian publication in the U.S. The Daughters of Bilitis lasted fourteen years, and printed their empowering mission statement on the inside cover of every issue of *The Ladder*.

1. Education of the variant . . . to enable her to understand herself and make her adjustment to society . . . this to be accomplished by establishing . . . a library . . . on the sex deviant theme; by sponsoring public discussions . . . to be conducted by leading members of the legal, psychiatric, religious and other professions; by advocating a mode of behavior and dress acceptable to society.
2. Education of the public . . . leading to an eventual breakdown of erroneous taboos and prejudices . . .
3. Participation in research projects by duly authorized and responsible psychologists, sociologists, and other such experts directed towards further knowledge of the homosexual.
4. Investigation of the penal code as it pertains to the homosexual, proposal of changes, . . . and promotion of these changes through the due process of law in the state legislatures.

The Ladder's publication, however, grew in a different direction. Editors changed, and a newer editor, Barbara Grier, was interested in expanding the readership of the magazine, removing the words "A Lesbian Review" from the cover in order to attract more readers. She took the subscriber list from the San Francisco office so she could distribute *The Ladder* separate from the organization, and without the subscriber list the Daughters of Bilitis lost their main method of communication between chapters. The Daughters of Bilitis folded in 1970, and by 1972, *The Ladder* also ran out of money and ceased publication.

Despite coming to a tumultuous end, the Daughters of Bilitis succeeded in uniting hundreds of lesbians across the country and influencing dozens of other lesbian and feminist organizations.

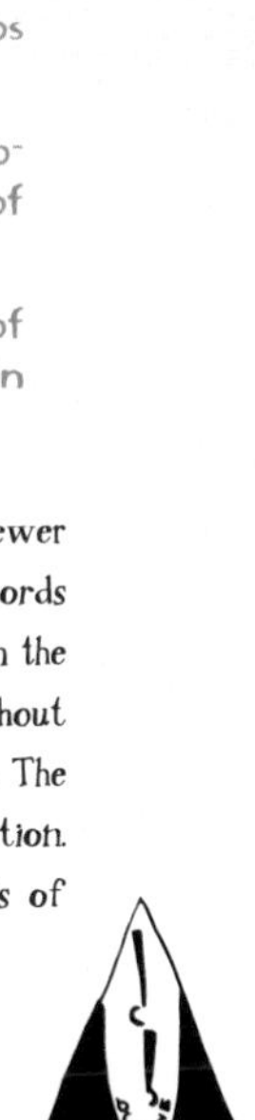

James Baldwin

AUGUST 2, 1924–DECEMBER 1, 1987

In 1956, James Baldwin published *Giovanni's Room*, a book that his publishers were reluctant to release due to its "controversial" homoerotic content. Baldwin grew up in Harlem, but eventually moved to France to escape the harsh racism and homophobia he experienced in the U.S. Once abroad, he began writing seriously on topics such as the social challenges and intersectionalities of being black and gay, as well as the internal struggles that men like him faced. *Giovanni's Room* laments his frustrations about his relationships with other men. His first American publisher refused to publish it, claiming that it would alienate readers due to its homosexual plot. Baldwin went on to write many more social commentaries—most notably *The Fire Next Time*, a book of essays that detail the issues of race and religion in his life—and was known for his activism. At the height of the AIDS epidemic, Baldwin spoke out about prejudice against homosexuals and the decriminalization of homosexuality: "Love is where you find it. No one has a right to try to tell another human being whom he or she can or should love." He died shortly after, but left behind a legacy in the hope for equality.

FRANK KAMENY

EQUALITY FOR HOMOSEXUALS

GAY IS GOOD

MAY 21, 1925–OCTOBER 11, 2011

In 1957, Frank Kameny, an astronomer for the U.S. Army Map Service, was publicly outed and thrust into unemployment due to the Lavender Scare. As he was unable to work in the United States federal government again, he devoted his life to the gay rights movement. Kameny appealed his firing, and although he lost the appeal, his proceeding became the first civil rights claim based on sexual orientation. He is known as one of the most significant gay rights activists because of his early activism and willingness to address the issues faced by his community head-on, even though that was not the norm at the time. Kameny also participated in many major protests and dedicated his life to activism after his court case. The United States government eventually apologized for its mistreatment of Kameny and other gay activists. In 2009, John Berry, the director of the Office of Personnel Management, said, "In what we know today was a shameful action, the United States Civil Service Commission in 1957 upheld your dismissal from your job solely on the basis of your sexual orientation. . . . It is my duty and great pleasure to inform you that I am adding my support . . . for the repudiation of the reasoning of the 1957 finding by the United States Civil Service Commission to dismiss you from your job solely on the basis of your sexual orientation. Please accept our apology for the consequences of the previous policy of the United States government." Kameny accepted.

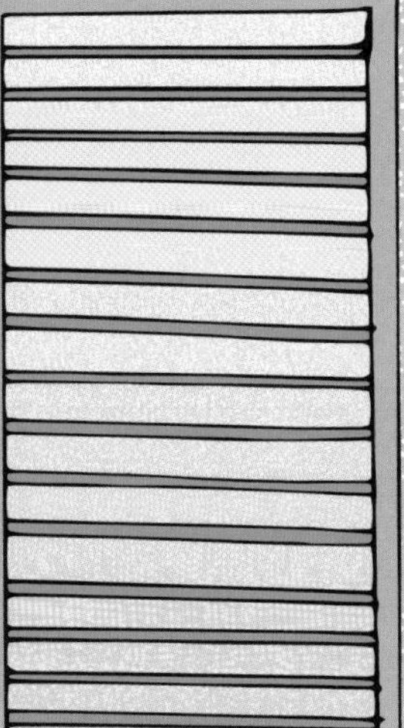

1959

One night in May 1959, in the neighborhood of Skid Row in Los Angeles, a small riot broke out when two cops attempted to raid and arrest some transgender folks at Cooper Do-nuts. The store was located between two gay bars, making it a prime spot to catch transgender or cross-dressing people hanging out. Back then, it was grounds for arrest if the gender stated on your ID and your presented gender did not seem to match up. The police were literally the fashion police in this case. When the two cops couldn't fit all the people they wanted to arrest in the back of the cop car, people started throwing coffee and trash at the police, driving them away. Once they were gone, people began rioting in the streets and more police came. Several arrests were made. It is said that this incident helped launch the beginning of the gay

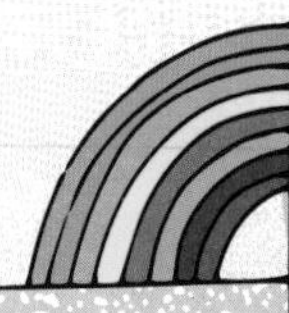

rights movement, and of course it did! Any queer person fighting against the homophobic establishment, no matter how small the situation, is taking a step toward becoming visible in a world that has tried so hard to categorize the LGBTQ+ community as "invalid."

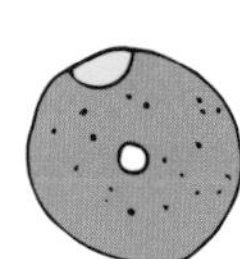

THE CASTRO DISTRICT BAYARD RUSTIN THE REJECTED ILLINOIS REPEALS SODOMY LAWS HOMOSEXUALITY: A PSYCHO-ANALYTIC STUDY OF MALE HOMOSEXUALS BOB DAMRON'S ADDRESS BOOK SAMUEL STEWARD POLICE RAIDS U.S. ARMY PROTESTS THE BLACK CAT COMPTON'S CAFETERIA RIOTS THE ADVOCATE OSCAR WILDE MEMORIAL BOOKSHOP METROPOLITAN COMMUNITY CHURCH ANDY WARHOL AUDRE LORDE THE STONEWALL RIOTS GAY LIBERATION FRONT

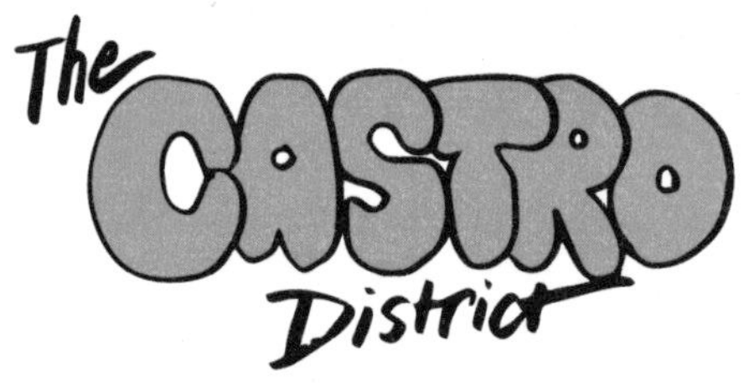

SAN FRANCISCO, CA

Once known as Eureka Valley, the Castro (renamed after one of the main streets going through the area) started to grow into the gay neighborhood that it is today in the 1960s. Its original residents began to move out to the suburbs of San Francisco, and a community of gay men were quick to snatch up the cheap real estate left behind. With the era of activism and resistance in effect, the gay community of the Castro kept growing. The Daughters of Bilitis's founders opened their first chapter in the area, and a Mattachine chapter opened in the late 1950s as well. From the opening of the Twin Peaks Tavern in the early seventies (the first gay bar with actual windows that allowed people to openly *see* gay people hanging out together), to gay pride marches and rallies, to the assassination of Harvey Milk in 1978 and the AIDS epidemic in the eighties, the community has come together through great times and hard times, creating a safe space and neighborhoods for queers of all sorts. It's important to remember that even San Francisco, one of the gayest cities ever, was once just as dangerous for gay people as anywhere else in the United States. Gay bars were raided by police, instilling fear in closeted gays. Nowadays, the Castro is quite the tourist destination, with its bright rainbow crosswalks and rainbow flags on every lamppost, not to mention many bars and restaurants, new and old. You can also find the Human Rights Campaign store and the GLBT Historical Society Museum here.

Bayard Rustin

MARCH 17, 1912–AUGUST 24, 1987

Bayard Rustin was one of the first openly gay black men in the homophobic and racist times of the 1940s, '50s, and '60s. Rustin worked hard to help shape the civil rights movement, and being an openly gay man made this challenge even more difficult. In the early fifties, Rustin was arrested for having sex with two men and spent sixty days in jail. He worked closely with Martin Luther King Jr. to help found the Southern Christian Leadership Conference; however, his sexuality became a point of conflict. Rustin and King worked together to plan the Montgomery bus boycott, but a reporter threatened to expose Rustin's sexuality in the press, so he was forced to back away from the boycott. While planning a march by blacks on the Democratic National Convention in 1960 in protest of John F. Kennedy's lackluster civil rights positions, Adam Clayton Powell Jr. threatened to tell the press that King and Rustin were having an affair, again forcing Rustin away from the movement. Bayard Rustin also helped to plan the historic 1963 March on Washington, but once again had to withdraw due to threats of exposure. Despite these setbacks, Rustin continued to publicly speak on the intersectionality between civil rights, gay rights, and human rights. He published an essay, "From Montgomery to Stonewall," that detailed the parallels between homophobia and racism. Rustin died in 1987, and received a posthumous Presidential Medal of Freedom in 2013, accepted by his partner, Walter Naegle.

The Rejected

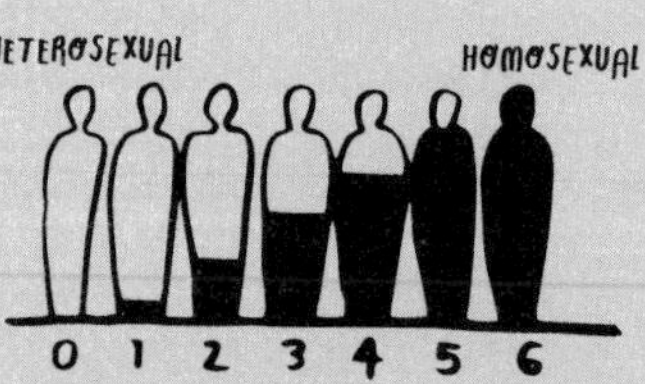

1961

The Rejected was a documentary film about homosexual men—the first of its kind broadcast on American public television. The concept was thought up by a producer, John W. Reavis, who wanted to give an objective view on homosexuals: Who were homosexuals, how did they get that way, what was their lifestyle, how were they treated, and how would they like to be treated? Reavis interviewed many subjects in a talk show format, showing stereotypes of homosexuality and then having his subjects discuss the stereotypes from their perspectives. Many experts weighed in, including anthropologist Margaret Mead, psychiatrist Karl Bowman, religious figureheads, and Mattachine Society president Hal Call. The film was critically well received and popular! After airing, the documentary was considered lost for many years, but eventually the original film was found and is currently archived in the Library of Congress.

Illinois Repeals Sodomy Laws

1961

Upon a revision of its criminal laws as a whole, Illinois became the first state to repeal sodomy laws. This meant that people could have consensual sex with their partners and not get arrested or criminally charged for it. Nineteen more states followed Illinois's lead over the following decade.

HOMOSEXUALITY

A PSYCHOANALYTIC STUDY OF MALE HOMOSEXUALS

1962

Homosexuality: A Psychoanalytic Study of Male Homosexuals was published by psychoanalyst Irving Bieber. The book was created as a counterpoint to the 1948 Kinsey Report, and asserted that homosexual men were created as the by-product of having smothering or seductive mothers and detached or rejecting fathers. At the time, the work was highly influential, and Bieber was regarded as an expert on homosexuality. Data for the book was gathered from nine psychologists who treated 106 male homosexuals. Over the course of treatment, these psychologists gathered information about the families of the patients, particularly their feelings about their mothers, fathers, siblings, and peers. They also asked patients about the effect that these figures had on their lives and memories of preferences and activities during their childhoods. Currently, *Homosexuality* is the most cited study justifying conversion therapy, which probably tells you something. Understandably, the study received a negative response from the gay movement. Activists argued that while the book was persuasive, it was generally unscientific and flawed. The conclusions were based on the psychologists' preconceived ideas, researcher bias, and stereotypes of masculinity. Some scientific and academic researchers supported the work, but many discredited it. The book remained the leading study on homosexuality until homosexuality was removed from the American Psychiatric Association's *Diagnostic and Statistical Manual of Mental Disorders* in 1973.

THE ADDRESS BOOK

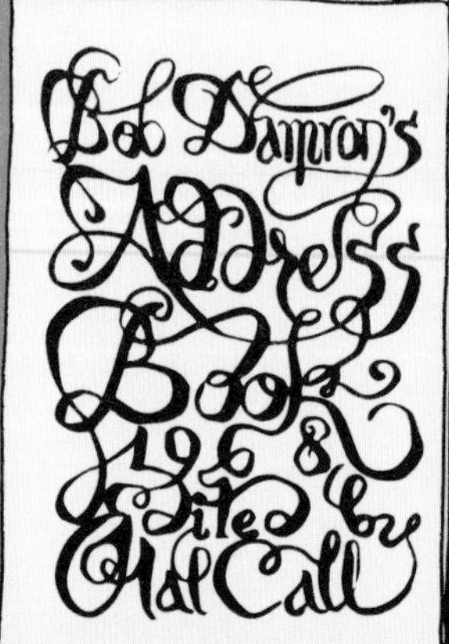

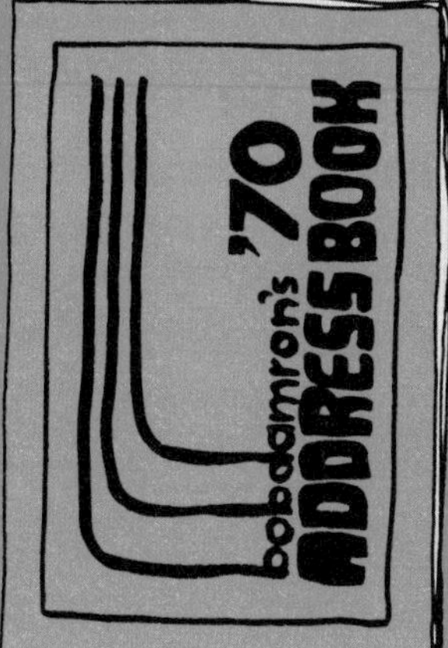

bob damron's

address book

'71

bd

BOB DAMRON'S

ADDRESS BOOK

'72

bd

BOB DAMRON'S

ADDRESS BOOK

'76

bd

BOB DAMRON'S

USA CANADA PUERTO RICO VIRGIN ISLANDS MEXICO

ADDRESS BOOK

'88

bd

BOB DAMRON'S

USA CANADA PUERTO RICO VIRGIN ISLANDS MEXICO

ADDRESS BOOK

'90

Bob Damron's ADDRESS BOOK

1964

Bob Damron was a pioneer in the LGBTQ+ travel realm. In 1964, Damron published the first-ever edition of *The Address Book*, a palm-sized booklet listing queer-friendly establishments across the United States, essentially providing a map for queers all over the country to find each other in restaurants, bars, and other businesses. This tiny travel guide is updated every year and is still being published to this day in book form and online. The concept of *The Address Book* has helped pave the way for many gay travel blogs and businesses, as well as location-based apps like Grindr.

"SEE AMERICA. FIND A FRIEND."

Samuel Steward

JULY 23, 1909–DECEMBER 31, 1993

Tattoos began to show up in the queer community in the sixties, as a means of secret communication and because Marlon Brando in *The Wild One* had made them hot. Samuel Steward—known by many names, including Philip Sparrow during his tattoo artist stint and Phil Andros as a gay pulp writer—became the official tattoo artist for Hells Angels in Oakland, California, and a leader in the early normalization of tattoos. He was mentor to Ed Hardy (yes, like the T-shirts that were popular in the late 2000s) and befriended Kenneth Anger, a well-known experimental filmmaker, among many other influential creatives. People in the leather community identified with the masculine essence that surrounded tattoos, making them popular among gay men, especially those who prided themselves on their masculinity.

In addition to having a mixed bag of hobbies and professions, Samuel also spent years contributing to Alfred Kinsey's human sexuality research.

POLICE
RAIDS
XXX

POLICE RAIDS

Many people know about the Stonewall Riots—and they know that the police raids of gay bars were targeted and violent. However, to understand the significance behind these raids, one must understand that most gay bars were not owned by fellow gays; they were owned by the Mafia. This was a mutually beneficial relationship that lasted throughout the sixties. Laws against homosexuality were still in effect in the 1960s in many states—in fact, it wasn't until 2003 that homosexuality became legal nationwide (though that story is a bit more nuanced).

In New York specifically, homosexuality was legal; however, establishments that served alcohol to gay customers would be cited as "disorderly," and the state liquor authority refused to issue liquor licenses to bars that frequently had reports of "disorderly conduct" (aka gay stuff). Mafia members, spotting a new business opportunity, began to control most of the gay bars in the West Village, a popular gay hangout area. They'd take ownership of a bar, then bribe the police precincts to turn a blind eye to it. Considering the need for a communal space in the gay community, the Mafia could count on earning back their bribe. The Stonewall Inn, operated by the Genovese crime family, was billed as a private "bottle club" and required patrons to sign in. The Mafia was able to use this sign-in system to extort and blackmail many of the bar's wealthier customers. Bars were raided despite police bribes, and the Mafia would often simply move the entire establishment to another location.

LGBTQ+ people have always had a tumultuous relationship with police, as police were mandated to enforce anti-LGBTQ+ laws. Again, almost every state had anti-sodomy laws, which made consensual sex between same-gender couples illegal. These laws put LGBTQ+ people in danger. At times, they would be beaten up by police, who claimed they were enforcing a "crime against nature" law. Additionally, gays didn't feel they could call on the cops for protection in an emergency, as they risked being either blamed or ignored. Relationships with police have improved, but that does not mean that homophobia and transphobia are not still rife in the law enforcement community. Trans people are still jailed in wrong-gender facilities. LGBTQ+ people are still being sexually assaulted in prisons.

Although this next section addresses the more well-known police raids—the Black Cat and Stonewall Inn—the history of abuse and terror from police against the LGBTQ+ community extends back for hundreds of years.

U.S. Army Protests

SEPTEMBER 14, 1964, AND APRIL 17, 1965

The first ever U.S. gay rights protest was held in front of the U.S. Army Building in New York City, organized by Randy Wicker, a gay rights activist, and members of the Homosexual League of New York and the New York City League for Sexual Freedom. The protest was aimed at the army's mistreatment of homosexuals, including dishonorable discharges and the release of gay men's records to employers. The New York City League for Sexual Freedom was made up of mostly heterosexuals preaching free love, and their joining of the picket in 1964 was one of the first instances of heterosexual support for gay rights. The picket received little to no attention, but it inspired Frank Kameny and fellow activist Jack Nichols to lead a second protest the following year.

The 1965 protest drew a slightly larger crowd and campaigned for equal treatment of gay employees, the repealing of sodomy laws, and the removal of homosexuality as a mental disorder in the *DSM-III*. The group consisted of members of the Mattachine Society and Daughters of Bilitis, and men dressed up in traditional suits and ties and women in dresses and heels to appear to fit in with the rest of mainstream society. The protest was not applauded by mainstream gay people, as many of them believed that they should keep quiet and not draw attention to themselves. Again, the protest drew little publicity, but the fact of it was significant; as Jack Nichols recalled, the demonstrators "stood up against the power structure, putting [their] bodies on the line. Nothing had happened except that we'd been galvanized, and, to a certain extent, immunized against fear." Following this protest, a number of other demonstrations occurred in the same year, in San Francisco and Philadelphia.

FIFTEEN MILLION
U.S. HOMOSEXUALS
PROTEST
FEDERAL TREATMENT
GOVERNMENT POLICY CREATES SECURITY RISKS
SEXUAL PREFERENCE IS IRRELEVANT TO EMPLOYMENT
GAY IS GOOD
65,000 Homosexual Sailors DEMAND NEW NAVY POLICY

THE BLACK CAT, LOS ANGELES

1966–67

In 1966, there were several bars in Silver Lake, Los Angeles, where gay men felt accepted; many gathered in the Black Cat on New Year's Eve to celebrate. A few minutes past midnight, policemen raided the bar in plain clothes, looking for signs of homosexual affection. They pulled bartenders and partygoers out into the night, arrested sixteen people, and charged six of them for lewd behavior. The men had been kissing. On February 11, 1967, hundreds of people showed up for the protest. At this point, it was the largest rally for gay rights that had ever occurred in the United States, though after the much larger protests and raids at Stonewall two years later, the West Coast protests were largely overshadowed.

Compton's Cafeteria Riots

1966

In August 1966, police showed up at Compton's Cafeteria, one of a chain of restaurants in San Francisco that were open 24/7. Located in the Tenderloin district, this location was one of the few places where transgender people could gather, as they were often unwelcome in gay bars. Many trans women found the sex work they needed to survive in the Tenderloin, having been kicked out of their homes or fired from jobs for their gender identities. Police would often come into the cafeteria and arrest trans people, under the pretense of their breaking the law by cross-dressing. Although the cafeteria was popular in the trans community, management often called the police to kick out loiterers. The trans community grew tired of the harassment—some had even been tossed around the back of a police van for simply wearing a shirt with the buttons on the wrong side. One night, instead of just letting themselves be arrested, some of the trans patrons fought back, throwing coffee, flipping tables, and swinging purses. Many were arrested that night, but it was the first known instance of queer resistance to police harassment. However, this riot was not widely covered by media and has often been glossed over in queer history, with most acknowledging Stonewall as the first uprising, and erroneously attributing that uprising to gay white men.

OHIO LEGALIZES SEX
ADVOCATE
GAYS 'SICK' NO MORE
ADVOCATE
Hollywood Crackdown
ADVOCATE

the Advocate

1967

The Advocate was established in 1967 as an LGBT-interest magazine, and remains the oldest and largest LGBTQ+ publication to this day, the only current one founded before the Stonewall riots. It was started as a newsletter after the police raids on the Black Cat in Los Angeles. The newsletter was sold for twenty-five cents in L.A. gay bars and struggled to hang on until 1974, when an investment banker from San Francisco bought the publication and turned it into a biweekly national news magazine. ***The Advocate*** still exists today, publishing ten print issues per year and acting as an online news and media source for the LGBTQ+ community.

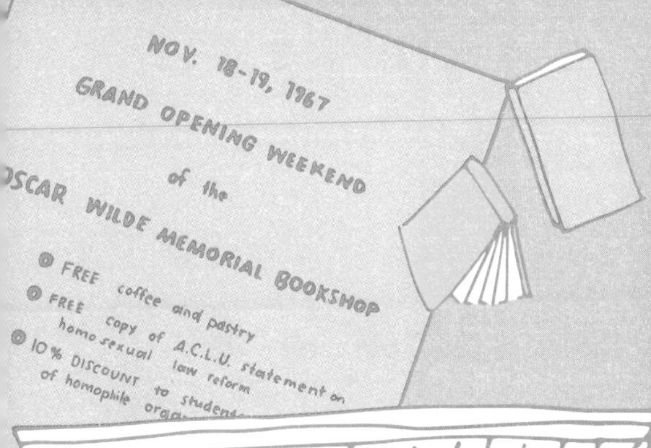

NOV. 18-19, 1967
GRAND OPENING WEEKEND
of the
OSCAR WILDE MEMORIAL BOOKSHOP
FREE coffee and pastry
FREE copy of A.C.L.U. statement on homosexual law reform
10% DISCOUNT to students of homophile

1967

The Oscar Wilde Memorial Bookshop opened in 1967 at 291 Mercer Street in New York City. It was the very first American bookstore devoted solely to gay and lesbian authors. Owner Craig Rodwell aimed to make it obvious that this store catered to gays and lesbians; the store carried Mattachine Society publications and provided a space for community gatherings, thereby making the society more accessible to the mainstream. He wanted to get the society to move out of secrecy and into the public eye. The shop became a staple for gays and lesbians, and the first pride parades were organized in its back room. The bookstore closed in 2009 due to financial difficulty, but paved the way for Giovanni's Room Bookstore in Philadelphia, named after James Baldwin's novel. Since its closing, Glad Day Bookshop in Toronto is the oldest surviving LGBTQ+ bookshop in North America.

GAY IS GOOD
CLOSED MONDAYS
"A BOOKSHOP OF THE HOMOPHILE YOUTH MOVEMENT"
Oscar Wilde Memorial Bookshop
291 MERCER STREET
(212) 673-3539
NEW YORK, N.Y. 10003
FRED SARGENT, MANAGER

TROY PERRY

JULY 27, 1940–PRESENT

In 1968, Troy Perry founded the Metropolitan Community Church, a church that seeks to affirm the LGBTQ+ community, in Los Angeles. Perry was interested in preaching and became a Baptist pastor at a young age, but when he expressed his attraction toward males, he was told to quell his desires. He married a woman, but could not suppress his homosexuality and was forced to leave the Baptist Church. His marriage dissolved and he was encouraged to retire from the pulpit. Perry did step away from religion for a while, but after a suicide attempt he felt that he needed to offer a place for gay people to worship God. He put an advertisement in *The Advocate* offering a church service for gays. Despite a small turnout, he continued these services, and they gradually grew in size. In 1971, the Metropolitan Community Church opened its own building with over a thousand members. Perry performed public same-sex unions and ordained women as pastors. Because of its outspoken and controversial views, the church was often targeted for arson; however, the Metropolitan Community Church continued to grow in membership and currently has over two hundred congregations in thirty-three countries.

PRESENT DAY LOCATION IN L.A.

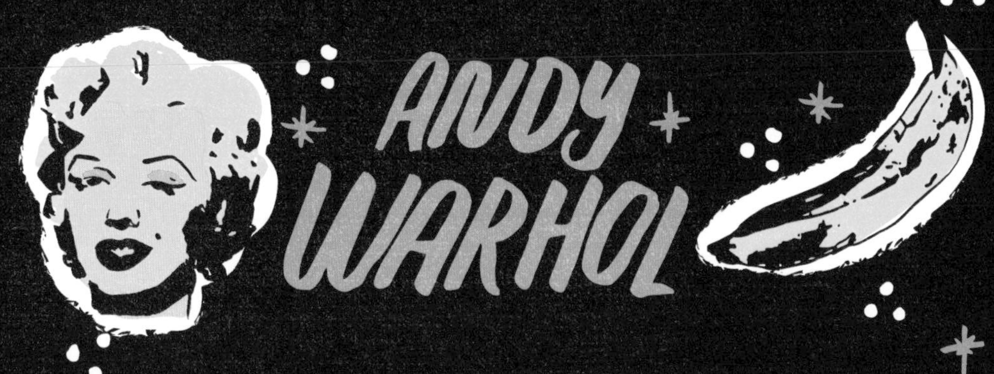

ANDY WARHOL

AUGUST 6, 1928–FEBRUARY 22, 1987

Andy Warhol was an American artist who guided the pop art movement. He is known for many popular works, including his silkscreens of Campbell's soup cans and Marilyn Monroe, and his film *Chelsea Girls*. As Warhol gained attention, he was seen as a controversial artist. His studio became a gathering place for eccentrics of all kinds, from intellectuals to drag queens. Warhol's career did not end with pop art: he managed the band the Velvet Underground and authored many books. Warhol was also open about his homosexuality before the gay liberation movement really took off. Warhol photographed and drew many male nudes, some of which were deemed "too gay" for fine art galleries. Warhol died in 1987 after complications following a gallbladder surgery.

Audre Lorde

FEBRUARY 18, 1934–NOVEMBER 17, 1992

Audre Lorde was a progressive powerhouse—a feminist, writer, and civil rights activist. Lorde explored the intersections of race, sex, sexuality, and class and did not hesitate to confront the injustices found in these identities. From an early age, she loved poetry; she published her first poem in high school. She remained in New York for college and graduate school, and eventually went to teach at Tougaloo College (a historically black college in Mississippi) where she openly acknowledged, articulated, and confronted her identity and place in society as a black woman (and eventually a queer woman). Lorde's poetry gained recognition when her collection *From a Land Where Other People Live* was nominated for a National Book Award. As Lorde's activism grew, she challenged the social stigmas surrounding being a black lesbian. She unceasingly challenged the whitewashed version of feminism that she saw many "radical" feminists practicing, arguing that this type of feminism increased the oppression of black women, while she sought to identify the underlying racism in feminism. Lorde was fierce in her ideals, asserting that *all* types of oppression were related. She celebrated all parts of her identity and acknowledged that they were all intertwined. Although Lorde died in 1992, her ideals contributed greatly to third-wave feminism, empowering women of color to critique the first- and second-wave feminist movements, which had downplayed the struggles and intersectionalities of sexual, racial, and class differences. Without a doubt, Lorde's activism has empowered generations of women and inspired courageous conversations and confrontations.

Women are powerful and dangerous.

the STONEWALL Riots

1969

The Stonewall riots were a series of violent demonstrations by members of the LGBTQ+ community after a police raid on the Stonewall Inn in the early hours of June 28, 1969. Like most gay bars, the Stonewall was operating under Mafia control in order to have a liquor license. The Stonewall was also different from other gay bars: most only allowed gay patrons, yet the Stonewall also allowed drag queens, runaways, and others. Marsha P. Johnson and Sylvia Rivera, two trans activists, were regulars! On June 28, police officers raided the bar and handcuffed gay patrons outside. As the crowd of patrons and bystanders grew, the interactions between police and the crowd became violent. Members of the LGBTQ+ community were beaten by officers, and supporters responded by throwing items at the officers. The raid culminated in the officers locking themselves inside the bar; the protesters responded by setting fire to their barricade. Although the crowd dispersed that night, over the next week demonstrations continued outside the bar, with thousands of others traveling to New York to express their support and solidarity. The Stonewall riots shifted the gay liberation movement into overdrive and inspired the community and its supporters to be more active and visible.

STONEWALL 20:

a generation of pride

STONEWALL

THE BAR CLUB BISTRO

JUNE 28 - 1969

GAY LIBERATION FRONT

1969

Directly following the events at the Stonewall, radical gays and lesbians in New York City banded together to form the Gay Liberation Front. With an "enough is enough" mentality, the GLF sought to end discrimination and oppression of the homosexual community through activism and political action. In February 1970, the GLF put out a statement in its newsletter saying, "The Gay Liberation Front is a militant coalition of radical and revolutionary homosexual men and women committed to fight the oppression of the homosexual as a minority group and to demand the right to the self-determination of our own bodies." In millennial speak, we're here, we're queer, and we don't want to be put in a box because of our sexual orientations and identities. The GLF's ideal was a world where everyone would be free of homophobia and sexism, and while there is still a ways to go, the group helped begin the revolution that is the gay rights movement. By openly fighting for the freedom of everyone to express their sexuality and identity, the GLF encouraged the beginning steps of normalizing queer people in society. Their activities were mainly hosted at Alternative U., a counterculture leftist school on Fourteenth Street and Sixth Avenue in NYC, where they threw weekly dances and other culture-building activities that brought gays and lesbians together in a safe and fun setting. The GLF picketed the *Village Voice* for refusing to print the word "gay" while advertising for one of their dance events, which became their first successful action.

"We are a revolutionary group of men and women formed with the realization that complete sexual liberation for all people cannot come about unless existing social institutions are abolished. We reject society's attempt to impose sexual roles and definitions of our nature."

1970s

CHRISTOPHER STREET LIBERATION DAY LAVENDER MENACE RUBYFRUIT JUNGLE HOMOSEXUALITY NO LONGER A MENTAL ILLNESS MARSHA P. JOHNSON SYLVIA RIVERA STREET TRANSVESTITES ACTION REVOLUTIONARIES MISS MAJOR GRIFFIN-GRACY LAMBDA LEGAL FREDDIE MERCURY CONGREGATION BEIT SIMCHAT TORAH THE LESBIAN HERSTORY ARCHIVES KATHY KOZACHENKO ROCKY HORROR PICTURE SHOW STUDIO 54 RENÉE RICHARDS THE RAINBOW FLAG DOE V. COMMONWEALTH ATTORNEY OF RICHMOND MARCH ON WASHINGTON HARVEY MILK A DIFFERENT LIGHT HANDKERCHIEF CODE DAVID BOWIE

CHRISTOPHER STREET Liberation Day

1970

Following the police raid at the Stonewall Inn on June 28, 1969, the LGBTQ+ community and their allies felt the need to use their voices and visibility to make a change. Eventually it was proposed that on the anniversary of the raid, supporters would hold an annual march. The proposal was radical: it called for no age limit, no dress code, no regulations. Before this, most LGBTQ+ activists would stick to traditional and nondisruptive demonstrations, with men wearing suits and ties and women wearing dresses, in order to fit in. The activist Brenda Howard met with Craig Rodwell, the founder of the Oscar Wilde Memorial Bookshop, and planned out the first ever NYC Pride Parade. The march was first known as the Christopher Street Liberation Day March but later switched to "Pride," based on the notion that while the LGBTQ+ community didn't have much power, they could always have their pride. Other cities—Chicago, Los Angeles, and San Francisco—followed suit and held their own pride parades. To this day, many cities hold their pride parades on or near the anniversary of the Stonewall riots, while other cities and countries throughout the world have created their own pride parades. Today, these parades not only celebrate pride, but acknowledge and mourn the violence and brutality that LGBTQ+ people have faced and still face.

LAVENDER MENACE

"What is a lesbian? A lesbian is the rage of all women condensed to the point of explosion."

1970

Betty Friedan, feminist, activist, and president of the National Organization for Women (NOW), called the presence of lesbians in the women's movement "the lavender menace." Friedan believed that lesbians would give feminists a bad reputation, associating the movement with, you know, man-hating radicals. Several lesbians, including author Rita Mae Brown, Karla Jay, Martha Shelley, Lois Hart, Barbara Love, Ellen Shumsky, Artemis March, Cynthia Funk, and Michela Griffo, many of whom were part of the Gay Liberation Front and would later call themselves the Radicalesbians, crashed the Second Congress to Unite Women in May 1970 (like, literally cut the lights in the auditorium where the event was being held and emerged in the darkness after outfit changes), protesting the exclusion of lesbians in the movement while dressed in T-shirts saying LAVENDER MENACE. They handed out copies of their manifesto, titled "The Woman Identified Woman," a piece explaining the connection between the male's role in society and how it acts as an oppressor specifically toward lesbian women in the world, and how heterosexual feminists' excluding lesbianism entirely is reflective of that same type of sexist behavior. It argues points such as how being a lesbian shouldn't be an "alternative" to dating and marrying men, and that marriage should be free of traditional sex roles and standards altogether. The manifesto's goal was to highlight that straight feminists' excluding lesbians from the movement reflected men's excluding women from parts of society, and was quite a double standard. It's actually a really on-point read, and we highly recommend checking it out, as it is (unfortunately) still pretty accurate in today's world.

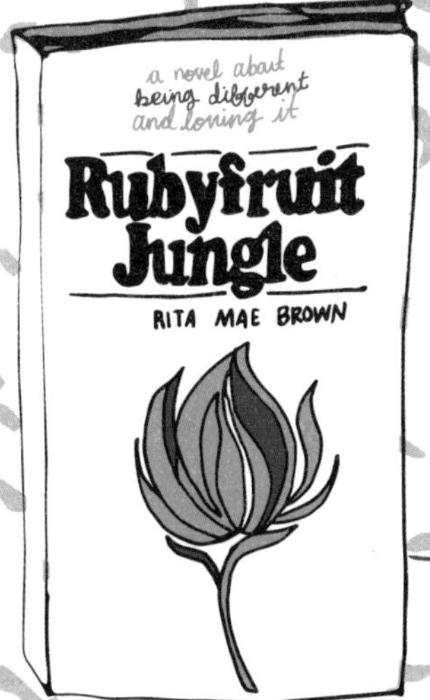

Rubyfruit Jungle

1973

Rubyfruit Jungle is a groundbreaking lesbian novel by Rita Mae Brown. A coming-of-age story about the protagonist, Molly Bolt, it mirrors Rita's own experiences as she explored her lesbian identity. The novel outlines Molly's struggles as she learns about herself through same-sex and opposite-sex relationships and her ultimate successes. The novel was as popular as it was controversial, making it one of the first commercially successful lesbian novels.

Homosexuality no longer a mental illness!

1973

In 1973, the American Psychiatric Association—the largest psychiatric organization in the world—stated that homosexuality was not a mental illness or sickness. In a panel organized by gay rights activist Barbara Gittings, Dr. H. Anonymous (later on revealed as John E. Fryer, M.D.) volunteered to speak on behalf of the gay members in the psychiatry community while in disguise. This statement was a huge milestone for the gay community, as many Americans viewed homosexuality as a perversion and illness. Mental illness has long been mischaracterized as something to hide, so classifying homosexuality as a mental illness made it even more taboo. The removal of homosexuality from the list of mental illnesses helped to shift the public's opinion on homosexuality. At this time, the APA was also one of the first groups to support civil rights legislation that ensured homosexuals their civil rights protections. They have continued to advocate for LGBTQ+ people, publicly opposing conversion therapy and Trump's transgender military ban.

pay it no mind.
Street Transvestites Action Revolutionaries

Marsha P. Johnson AUGUST 24, 1945–JULY 6, 1992

Marsha P. Johnson was a gay rights activist and popular drag queen in the New York City scene. She may have been considered trans or gender nonconforming, although these phrases were not widely used in her lifetime. She performed in the drag troupe Hot Peaches and was one of the first drag queens to go to Stonewall, as it was previously a bar only for gay men. Marsha was active in the Stonewall Inn riots—many say she was one of the ones to throw the first bricks. Following the riots, she joined the Gay Liberation Front, and in 1970, she and her friend Sylvia Rivera founded Street Transvestite Action Revolutionaries (STAR). Johnson and Rivera faced backlash from members of the LGBTQ+ community who were not interested in drag queens; however, Johnson and Rivera also both spoke about a third gender identity, a topic that had not been much explored at the time. Johnson continued her activism with ACT UP in the 1980s.

Like many others in the queer community, Marsha P. Johnson herself also struggled with homelessness and mental illness, often relied on sex work, and was arrested multiple times for prostitution. In 1992, her body was found in the Hudson River. Her death was ruled a suicide; however, there was doubt regarding whether she was suicidal, and many agreed that police were not interested in properly investigating her case because of her race and sexuality. Her death received little to no attention in the media. In 2012, transgender activist Mariah Lopez convinced the New York Police Department to reopen the case and investigate a possible homicide. Rest in power, Marsha.

Sylvia Rivera JULY 2, 1951–FEBRUARY 19, 2002

Sylvia Rivera was a drag queen and gay and transgender activist. Rivera battled substance abuse and often lived with a large homeless community. Despite her own struggles, Rivera fought tooth and nail for LGBTQ+ rights and spoke out for homeless LGBTQ+ youth. She was vocal and passionate about the systemic poverty and racism in the LGBTQ+ community. In the mid-1990s, she felt ostracized and marginalized by her own community, who were mostly focusing on assimilating into mainstream society. But toward the end of her life, Rivera renewed her activism, notably fighting for transgender people to be included in New York State's Sexual Orientation Non-Discrimination Act, and doggedly sought justice for Amanda Milan, a transgender woman murdered in New York City in 2000. Sylvia Rivera died in 2002 from complications of liver cancer. She lives on through the Sylvia Rivera Law Project, an organization that aims to "guarantee that all people are free to self-determine gender identity and expression, regardless of income or race, and without facing harassment, discrimination, or violence."

Street Transvestites Action Revolutionaries 1970

Street Transvestite Action Revolutionaries (STAR) was an organization that aimed to provide housing and support to gay, gender-nonconforming, and transgender youth and sex workers. STAR was the first group of its kind in the queer liberation movement. The first version of the house was a trailer in Greenwich Village, but the organization quickly found that they needed a more permanent space, and worked to rent a dilapidated four-bedroom apartment in the East Village. STAR House was only active for one year, but influenced many future radical queer spaces.

MISS MAJOR
GRIFFIN-GRACY

OCTOBER 25, 1940–PRESENT

Miss Major Griffin-Gracy is a trans activist and former director of the Transgender Gender Variant Intersex Justice Project, which assists incarcerated trans people. Growing up in Chicago, Miss Major questioned her gender identity, and came out as transgender in her teen years in the late fifties. Because transgender people were widely unheard of at the time, she relied on the black market for hormones and did sex work to support herself. Miss Major moved to New York City, where she became a staple in the LGBTQ+ community and a regular at the Stonewall Inn—in fact, she was present when the bar was raided. During the riots, Miss Major was taken into police custody, where she was abused by corrections officers. Like many LGBTQ+ individuals who relied on sex work and theft to stay alive, Miss Major was again arrested, for burglary, shortly after the Stonewall clash. She served five years in a men's prison, where she bonded with another prisoner, Frank "Big Black" Smith, who respected her gender identity and treated her as a woman even though she was forced to be grouped with men. He inspired her to address the problems of trans marginalization within the LGBTQ+ community, and when she was released, she moved to San Diego to address these issues. She began with a food bank and later moved to support trans women who were incarcerated or homeless. Miss Major fiercely defended trans people, knowing that they faced intense discrimination—saying "we only have each other," since trans people could not rely on police or other community supports. Miss Major continues to provide mentorship and activism for young trans people.

LAMBDA LEGAL

1973

Lambda Legal is a civil rights organization, formed in 1971 in New York, that focuses on the rights of the LGBTQ+ community. Its original incorporation was denied due to the nature of its proposed activities, but this denial was overturned in 1973. Lambda Legal has represented plaintiffs in many gay rights cases, including *Lawrence v. Texas*, which overturned sodomy laws in the U.S.

SEPTEMBER 5, 1946–NOVEMBER 24, 1991

Freddie Mercury was a singer and songwriter best known for his work with the flamboyant rock band Queen. He had an amazing four-octave vocal range and is considered one of the most renowned singers of all time. His performances were highly theatrical: Freddie often wore extravagant outfits, including tights and suspenders, and would perform with a broken microphone stand in his hand while dancing. While he never publicly acknowledged or confirmed his sexuality, there was a lot of speculation about it due to his flamboyant performances. He had a longstanding relationship with Mary Austin and publicly claimed his love and adoration for her: he said she was his only true friend. Toward the end of his life, he began a long-term relationship with Jim Hutton, who cared for him until he died. Mercury was diagnosed with AIDS in 1987, and by 1990 he became visibly gaunt and sickly. He did not confirm his status until two days before his death, when he made a public statement asking for privacy. He died on November 24, 1991.

Congregation Beit Simchat Torah

1973

Congregation Beit Simchat Torah was founded in New York City by Jacob Gubbay, a gay Jewish man who saw an ad for a gay Passover seder at a church in Chelsea in 1973. He met a group of other gay Jewish men at this ceremony, and they began to pray together weekly. Over the next few years, the congregation gained momentum, and by 1976 they moved into a loft in Greenwich Village, where they remained for forty years. As the AIDS crisis began to spread, the congregation lost hundreds of members, and began their search for a rabbi to provide chaplaincy for the ill and their families. They landed on a lesbian, Rabbi Sharon Kleinbaum. After this official assignment, the synagogue grew monumentally. The 1992 High Holiday services were conducted at the Jacob K. Javits Convention Center and were attended by over two thousand people—the largest gathering of lesbian and gay Jews in history. In 2011, after even further growth, the congregation purchased a larger building in Midtown that remains a safe space for the LGBTQ+ community to this day.

RAINBOW DOORWAY AT THE 151 BANKER STREET LOCATION

קהלה קדושה בית שמחת תורה

The Lesbian Herstory Archives

1974

After the Stonewall riots, gay liberation and activism skyrocketed. A group of LGBTQ+ academics founded the Gay Academic Union in 1973. After a year, many of the lesbian members of the group split off to form their own archive, a safe space where they could ensure that their herstory was told with their own voices, without sexist interference. The motto of the archives emphasizes this need to preserve herstory: "In memory of the voices we have lost." This collection has been maintained and preserved by lesbians and remains a community space for women. The archives began in the apartment of the founder, Joan Nestle, but eventually outgrew the space and moved to a brownstone in Park Slope, Brooklyn, in 1990. Currently, it houses over eleven thousand books and thirteen hundred periodicals, as well as an astounding number of buttons, T-shirts, photographs, zines, videos, and other lesbian memorabilia. The archives are open to the public for viewing and volunteering.

THE FOUNDERS

ARCHIVED DOCUMENTS

LIBRARY COLLECTION

SMILE
IF YOU'RE
A
LESBIAN

WE LOVE OUR DYKES
GAY IS GO

Kathy Kozachenko

1954–PRESENT

While many recall Harvey Milk as the first openly gay candidate to run for office, they overlook Kathy Kozachenko, a lesbian from Michigan who was elected to the Ann Arbor City Council on April 2, 1974. Kozachenko ran on the Human Rights Party platform (similar to the Democratic platform, but a bit more progressive). She served for two years before leaving politics and going to work in activism. Although her election *would* have been groundbreaking for the LGBTQ+ community, it was barely publicized. Much to her frustration, the day after the election, the *New York Times* glossed over her victory and eventually described her as a University of Michigan student first, and a lesbian last.

VOTE HRP
Human Rights Party
KOZACHENKO
2ND WARD
HRP

Rocky Horror Picture Show

1975

The Rocky Horror Picture Show is a cult classic musical movie that is essentially about gender-nonconforming pansexual aliens living in a spaceship castle on Earth and singing catchy tunes while taking turns hooking up with each other and their earthling guests, Brad (Barry Bostwick) and Janet (Susan Sarandon, who, by the way, is an incredible advocate and ally). AND IT'S AMAZING. Originally a small London show written by Richard O'Brien (who also plays Riff Raff the handyman in the musical), this film is a playful and peculiar masterpiece of the seventies, its main character the tall, handsome Dr. Frank-N-Furter (played by Tim Curry), who dresses completely in drag. Queers flocked to this film when it came out; its campiness, its fluid story line, and the fact that it's a MUSICAL made the community want to claim it for their own. Even in the present day, people attend live screenings of this movie, oftentimes reading from a script while actors pantomime the movie as it plays on-screen behind them. People dress in drag and lingerie and have a grand ol' time. Although the terms used in the actual film are outdated—like "transvestite" and "transsexual"—it still has a special place in the hearts of drag folks and people questioning their sexuality alike.

STUDIO 54

1977

Masterminds Steve Rubell and Ian Schrager met in college and eventually decided to go into business together after Steve's steak house failed and Ian jumped in to save the day. While defending Steve in court, Ian grew to respect his ambition, and the two began to bounce around the idea of opening a nightclub together. The space they bought at West Fifty-Fourth Street and Eighth Avenue in New York was originally an opera house, and later a studio for CBS. The boys opened Studio 54 on April 26, 1977, sending out invitations to the hottest celebrities at the time, many of whom showed up to party and dance. Studio 54 quickly became a place that everyone wanted to be, making headlines and buzz. It was a pretty exclusive club, hard to get into if you didn't fit the criteria at the door; even celebrities were occasionally charged an entrance fee. Since the club was in the former CBS studio, lots of props had been repurposed with lighting magic for entertainment during the club nights. The architecture and decor of the club maintained a lot of the integrity of the space itself, keeping studio fixtures and the stage, with a dance floor surrounded by pockets of comfy furniture for when you needed a break from dancing. There were often grand performances and shows, creating an exciting and extravagant vibe. Gay and transgender culture influenced a large part of Studio 54, since Steve Rubell was gay himself. Drag queens frequented the club, the bartenders and busboys sported short shorts with no shirts, and everyone was dancing with everyone all the time. Studio 54 encouraged letting loose, taking drugs, and having sex.

The IRS raided the club on December 14, 1978, based on suspicion of a cash-skimming and drug-dealing operation. There were millions of dollars of unaccounted-for cash hidden in the club, and upon discovery, Rubell and Schrager were charged with tax evasion. The two eventually pleaded guilty, and Studio 54 held its last party in February 1980 (the club reopened in 1981 and then stayed open for several more years). During and after its initial thirty-three-month run, it became legendary in New York nightlife. Rubell died of AIDS in 1989, at the age of forty-five, and Schrager went on to design hotels. He was recently pardoned by President Obama at the recommendation of the Studio 54 prosecutor. Although Studio 54, in all its glory, was only in operation for a short period of time, it helped in creating a safe and accepting environment in the late seventies for anyone (who could get in) who needed a place to just DANCE.

Renée Richards

AUGUST 19, 1934–PRESENT

Renée Richards became the first transgender person to compete in professional sports. From a young age, Richards was a talented athlete, competing on football, baseball, tennis, and swim teams. By the time she entered college, she was considered one of the best players in the country, and ranked high among male tennis players. However, during college she began to explore her female persona, despite the fact that transgenderism was considered a mental illness and rarely talked about openly. She began to see a doctor who started her on hormone injections, and eventually sought out sex-reassignment surgery to complete her transition. Between her college and transition years, Richards was not an active athlete, but she was encouraged by friends to compete at the U.S. Open in 1976. When the U.S. Tennis Association discovered her gender reassignment, they implemented a new policy that required a chromosome check to verify players' biological sex. Of course, Richards fought this policy tooth and nail, and consequently was not able to play in any professional league. She sued the United States Tennis Association, asserting that she had been the victim of discrimination and arguing that the acceptance of her gender reassignment would signify a radical change in accepting transgenderism. The tennis association argued that others would follow suit and undergo gender reassignment in order to play in the women's league. The case made its way to the New York Supreme Court, and in 1977 the judge ruled in her favor. He argued that Renée Richards, despite being born a man, was now a female, and to require her to pass a chromosomal test to prove her sex would be discriminatory and a violation of her civil rights. Richards continued her tennis career, after joining the women's professional circuit, until 1981, when she retired at age forty-seven. Her Supreme Court case was one of the first victories in transgender rights.

The Rainbow Flag

1977

Gilbert Baker, a Kansan gay activist and former U.S. Army member, was challenged by Harvey Milk to create a symbol of pride for the gay community in 1974; four years later, the rainbow flag was revealed at the 1978 San Francisco pride parade. While not confirmed, it's been suggested that Baker may have been inspired by Judy Garland's version of "Over the Rainbow"—Garland being one of the first gay icons. After Harvey Milk's assassination in 1978, there was a huge jump in demand for the flag. The original design contained two extra stripes, hot pink and turquoise; however, at the time the specialized hot-pink fabric was not widely available, so the rainbow flags began to be sold without the additional stripe. One year later, the flag was again modified as the city found that once they began hanging the flag from lampposts, one of the stripes was obscured by the pole. The turquoise stripe was dropped, and the six-color version (red, orange, yellow, green, blue, violet) was popularized. Since its inception, many variations have been used—flags with an additional two colors, brown and black, have also been popularized to represent inclusion.

TRADITIONAL FLAG

ORIGINAL FLAG

PHILADELPHIA FLAG

Doe v. Commonwealth Attorney of Richmond

1976

Doe v. Commonwealth Attorney of Richmond was a 1976 Supreme Court decision that upheld Virginia's ban on homosexual sodomy. It was the first Supreme Court decision that dealt with homosexual sodomy. Virginia's case was built on a long history—in 1610, shortly after the first English colony was established in Jamestown, the state adopted England's sodomy laws; however, homosexual men were not singled out by these laws. In fact, the first person punished under them was a woman. By the 1970s, gay subculture had grown significantly in cities, and gatherings of homosexual men became police targets; raids of known gay hangouts were commonplace. This court case was filed on the coattails of Roe v. Wade, in hopes that a similar "right to privacy" might be found to extend to homosexuals. In Roe v. Wade, the plaintiffs had argued that privacy was greater than morality—the state had no right to invade privacy in order to promote a moral objection to abortion. Despite the effort to draw on the public's move toward a more progressive look at civil rights, the court upheld the anti-sodomy law and claimed that it was constitutional.

March on Washington

OCTOBER 14, 1979

Although there had been many other, smaller organized protests by the LGBTQ+ community, this march was the first national gay rights demonstration. After Milk's assassination in 1978, the LGBTQ+ community became more galvanized, and this began to unify the smaller LGBTQ+ groups. The goal of the march was to add discrimination against sexual orientation to the Civil Rights Act of 1964 and to allow gays and lesbians to serve in the military and in federal jobs. While the march did not bring about immediate change—we have yet to ban discrimination based on sexual orientation—it did bring together a previously fragmented community, showing the country its power and size.

THE CLOSET IS AN AWFUL PLACE TO DIE
NATIONAL MARCH FOR LESBIAN AND GAY RIGHTS
OCT. 14
WE ARE EVERYWHERE

Harvey Milk

MAY 22, 1930–NOVEMBER 27, 1978

Harvey Milk became the first openly gay elected official in California when he was elected to serve on San Francisco's Board of Supervisors in 1977. On the Board of Supervisors, Milk worked under George Moscone, who was an early supporter of gay rights and abolished the city's anti-sodomy law. As Milk's popularity grew, he spoke out on issues of interest to LGBTQ+ people, women, minorities, and other marginalized communities. On November 27, 1978, a disgruntled former supervisor assassinated Milk and Mayor Moscone. Despite his untimely death, Milk blazed a trail for other LGBTQ+ individuals to run for public office and ultimately increased visibility for LGBTQ+ individuals, believing that the more people who came out of the closet, the more their families and friends would support protections for equal rights.

A DIFFERENT LIGHT

1979

A Different Light was a four-bookstore chain for the LGBTQ+ community that opened in Los Angeles in 1979 and eventually added three other locations: one more in Los Angeles, one in San Francisco, and one in New York City. A Different Light was more than just a bookstore: it hosted events, art shows, reading groups, discussions, and much more, and served as a much-needed social center for organization. Although the bookstores eventually went under, their original mission of spreading LGBTQ+ literature into the mainstream was a success. By the mid-nineties, most larger bookstores, like Barnes & Noble, began to stock an LGBTQ+ section. The last store to close, the San Francisco branch, in 2011, fell amid a wave of LGBTQ+ bookstore closings, including the Oscar Wilde Memorial Bookshop in New York and Lambda Rising in D.C.

HANDKERCHIEF code

While it's unknown exactly where and when the "hanky code" started, many believe its origin was in the early 1970s, when a *Village Voice* journalist joked that it would be easier to wear a hanky in your pocket than tell your partner what kind of sex you prefer. Some claim that it even dates back to San Francisco after the Gold Rush, when men would fulfill their need to square dance by wearing a coded hanky in their pocket to indicate if they'd dance the women's part or the men's part. Now, it's either a cute fashion statement or perhaps a nod to the past.

DAVID BOWIE

JANUARY 8, 1947–JANUARY 10, 2016

David Bowie was a British-born musician who changed the game when it came to stage presence and expression. His performances were often done in wild outfits that ranged from futuristic spaceman to androgynous disco drag, if that's even a thing. Bowie helped bring visibility to the queer community through his rock 'n' roll, starting with Ziggy Stardust, all the way until his passing in 2016. Although Bowie claimed to be both gay and bisexual, labels are trash sometimes, and he wasn't one for them. Being a glittery and inspiring idol to queers everywhere, Bowie truly left a mark on this community despite not being a traditional activist.

1980s

PFLAG HUMAN RIGHTS CAMPAIGN WISCONSIN ANTI-DISCRIMINATION LAW THE LIMELIGHT WIGSTOCK ANNIE ON MY MIND GLAAD GLBT HISTORICAL SOCIETY DEAR ABBY NATIONAL COMING OUT DAY THE AIDS CRISIS PUBLIC PERCEPTION GOVERNMENT RESPONSE AIDS MEMORIAL QUILT ACT UP AND THE BAND PLAYED ON KEITH HARING MADONNA

PARENTS
&
PFLAG
FRIENDS OF LESBIANS AND GAYS
PFLAG was founded in 1973 by parents who really loved their gay son

1980

The idea for Parents and Friends of Lesbians and Gays began way back in 1972, when Jeanne Manford marched with her son in the New York City pride parade. She found that many other LGBTQ+ people needed her to help their parents understand them, and decided to start a support group. The first meeting in 1973 began small, with about twenty parents in attendance. Similar groups sprouted across the country, and by 1980 the organizations meshed and began to promote themselves by distributing information to the general public. By 1981, PFLAG was established as a national organization in Los Angeles. The organization grew from there, helping pass legislation, bringing awareness to LGBTQ+ hate crimes, protecting LGBTQ+ students, and much more. Although the organization officially goes by the acronym "PFLAG," it includes bisexual and trans people as well.

Human Rights Campaign

1980

The Human Rights Campaign actually began as the Human Rights Campaign Fund, an organization with the intent of fund-raising to support LGBTQ+-friendly candidates who would push for gay civil rights and legislature. Founded in 1980 by Steve Endean, the HRCF quickly expanded, celebrating many victories in the years to come. By the 1990s, the HRCF wanted to grow beyond raising funds for gay-friendly politicians to providing support and education, and fighting for issues directly as an organization. The "Fund" was dropped from its title, although it is still involved in political lobbying and fund-raising. The HRC's current logo is the iconic blue square and yellow equals symbol. The HRC has helped fight for marriage equality, the Don't Ask, Don't Tell repeal, nondiscrimination against the queer community, and much more.

Wisconsin Anti-Discrimination Law

1982

On February 25, 1982, Wisconsin passed a law preventing discrimination based on sexual orientation. It was the first state to do so by a decade. More than ten years after the Stonewall riots, LGBTQ+ people were still being denied jobs and housing based on their sexual identity. Many members of the community chose to hide their sexuality in order to keep their sense of security. This Wisconsin bill, drafted by Democratic politician Lloyd Barbee and eventually signed into law by Governor Lee S. Dreyfus, stated that one cannot be denied housing, accommodations, or employment based upon one's sexuality. Although this bill was a triumph for the community, it did not explicitly protect members of the trans community, who continue to go unprotected. Despite many states eventually following suit, there is still no federal law against discrimination on the basis of sexual orientation or gender identity.

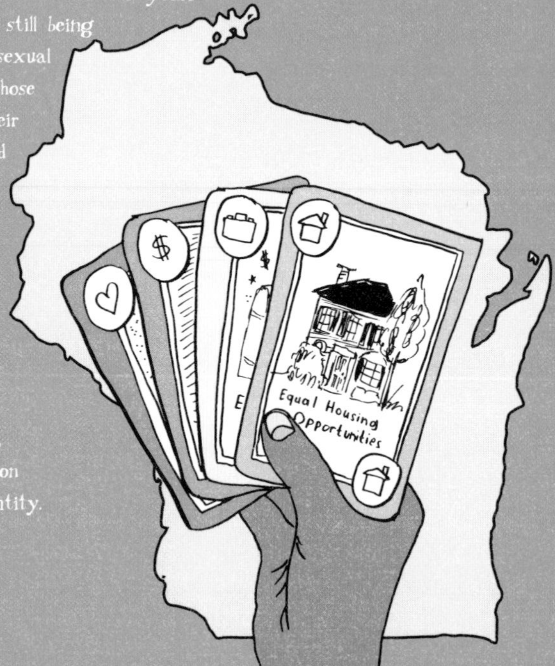

the LIMELIGHT

1983

Built in 1852, this Gothic Revival former Episcopalian church on the corner of Twentieth Street and Sixth Avenue in the Chelsea neighborhood of New York City is an ideal example of the ever-changing culture in the city, in building form. From a church, to a cultural center, to a rehabilitation center, nightclub, gym, boutique shopping mall, and restaurant, the Limelight has been through it all. In 1983, nightclub enthusiast Peter Gatien won the property in a bidding war from the previous owners and charged full speed ahead with creating one of the most influential clubs in the 1980s queer scene. Its opening party in November 1983 was hosted by pop artist Andy Warhol and included A-list celebrities among its guests. Frequented by drag queens and partygoers alike, the Limelight had a very diverse clientele, aiding in the birth of the "club kid" scene. To be a club kid was to dress to shock, showing up to raves and underground parties in the most outrageous and overdone garb that the eighties and nineties could offer. The fashion trends brought on by the influencers of the nightclub era helped shape the nightclub scene then and still influence drag today. However, drugs were a huge part of the deal. At the time, ecstasy and heroin were making their way through the dance scenes. The Limelight hit the news in 1994 when club promoter Michael Alig murdered Angel Melendez, a drug dealer at the Limelight. Alig and Melendez were immortalized in James St. James's memoir about the whole fiasco, *Disco Bloodbath*. Gatien soon fell under suspicion of running a drug ring in the club, and the Limelight began its decline. After changes of name and ownership, the club eventually shut down in 2007.

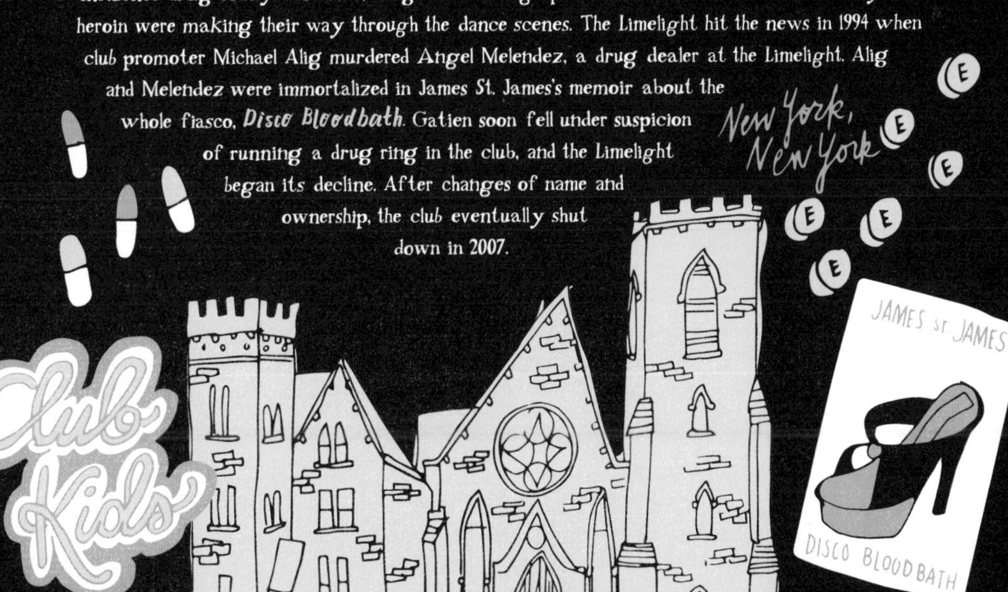

1984

In the East Village in Manhattan in the early 1980s, Wigstock started as an impromptu drag performance in the park and turned into a yearly festival that celebrated drag performance. It was held on and off for two decades, always taking place on Labor Day. Wigstock was a special gathering that brought crowds together for a day of performances by many local NYC drag queens. Lady Bunny, its founder, describes Wigstock as an "outrageous drag festival of drag [*sic*] and music which electrified New Yorkers every Labor Day for over 20 years."

Annie on My Mind

1982

Annie on My Mind is a novel by Nancy Garden following a romantic relationship between two girls, Annie and Liza. It is a typical coming-of-age story, with both Annie and Liza struggling to navigate their feelings for each other and the pressures of being a teenager (falling in love, pleasing your parents, choosing a college, the works!). The two share a romantic attraction, and are eventually outed. Despite being well received (it made the 1982 *Booklist* Reviewer's Choice, the 1982 American Library Association Best Books, and the ALA Best of the Best lists), the book stirred up controversy in Kansas City when copies were donated to high schools in the area. Parents objected to the content and the books were burned. The controversy continued, with the Kansas City School District superintendent removing the book from high school libraries more than ten years later, in 1993. The case went to U.S. District Court two years after that; the judge ruled that a school needn't purchase the book, but it cannot pull the book from shelves unless it is educationally unsuitable, which *Annie on My Mind* was not.

GLAAD

1985

GLAAD was founded in New York City in 1985 by a small group of writers and journalists in response to the homophobic and negative representation of HIV, AIDS, and the queer community in the media. In 1987, GLAAD was victorious in pushing the *New York Times* to print the word "gay" in reference to queers, rather than "homosexual." Chapters spread to the West Coast, where members advocated for proper queer representation in Hollywood. Once "GLAAD" stood for "Gay & Lesbian Alliance Against Defamation," but the organization became simply "GLAAD" in later years to be inclusive toward transgender and bisexual people, and, you know, anyone else who falls under the queer umbrella! As time went on and technology, news, and social media evolved, so did GLAAD. While it started with protests against newspapers and other publications, GLAAD now works in the realm of the Internet, helping create safe spaces for queer people everywhere. The organization has campaigned for custom gender and pronoun options on Facebook, trans-inclusive updates to Tinder, and so on. It has also helped change the lingo used around queer people to more positive words, denouncing outdated and derogatory terms, like "transsexual," for example. The GLAAD platform is huge now, with support from other organizations, celebrities, and people in the media all pushing for acceptance of the LGBTQ+ community.

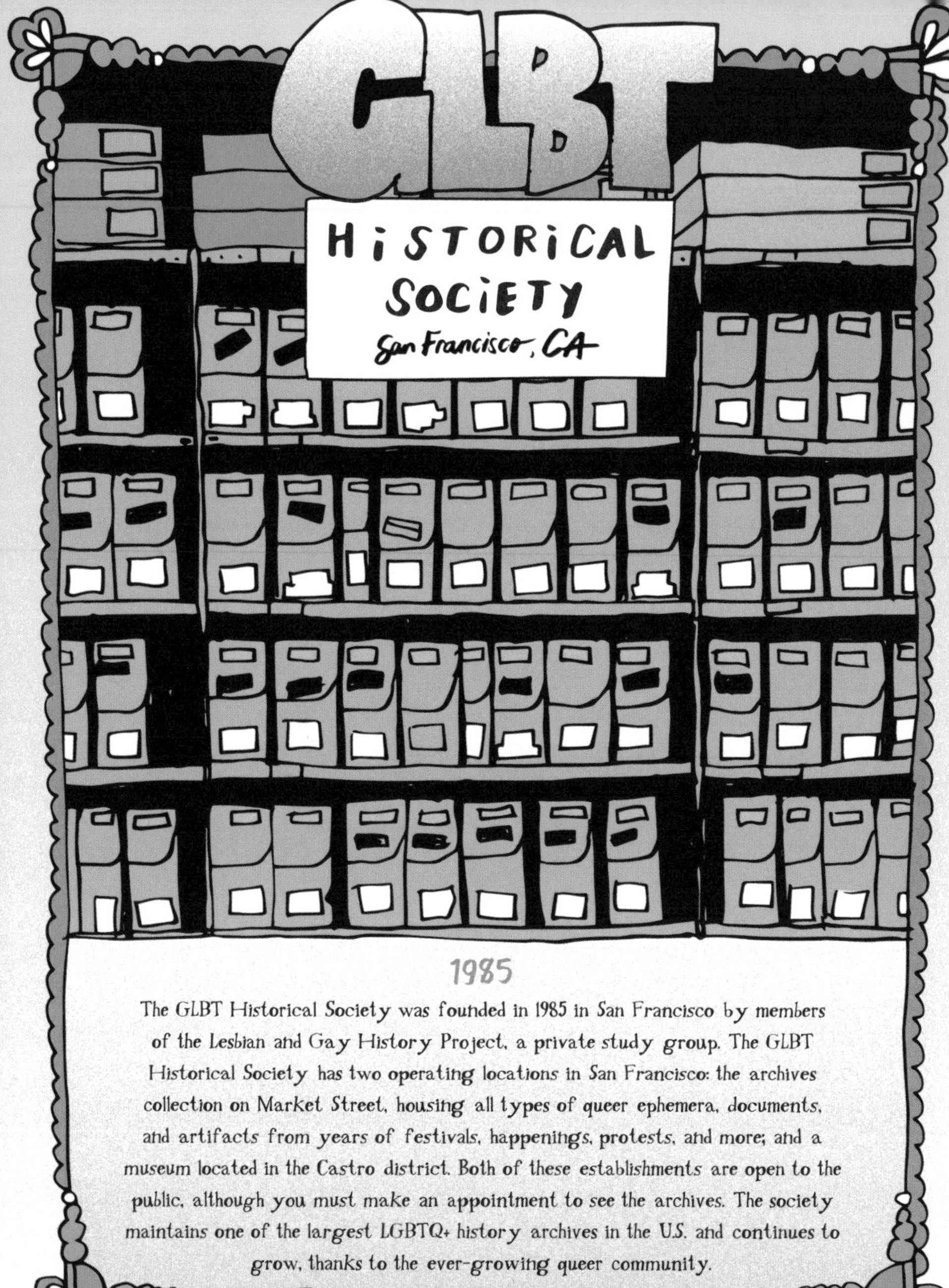

1985

The GLBT Historical Society was founded in 1985 in San Francisco by members of the Lesbian and Gay History Project, a private study group. The GLBT Historical Society has two operating locations in San Francisco: the archives collection on Market Street, housing all types of queer ephemera, documents, and artifacts from years of festivals, happenings, protests, and more; and a museum located in the Castro district. Both of these establishments are open to the public, although you must make an appointment to see the archives. The society maintains one of the largest LGBTQ+ history archives in the U.S. and continues to grow, thanks to the ever-growing queer community.

DEAR ABBY:

Surprising Gay Icon!

1960S–PRESENT

Dear Abby is a surprising gay icon! With her famed advice column, Abby influenced how parents felt about their gay children, how gay people felt about themselves, and how gay people thought about other gay people. In a time before social media, finding others with shared identities and experiences was much harder. Many turned to advice columns, and "Dear Abby" was arguably the most famous. Beginning in the sixties and seventies, Dear Abby found herself getting a lot of mail asking for advice about topics surrounding homosexuality. Dear Abby always responded in support of gays, which was huge in this time, as many still considered homosexuality a sickness and a perversion. In fact, PFLAG credits Dear Abby with bringing the group national attention, after she referenced the organization in response to a parent's question about their gay child. Sassy and charismatic, Dear Abby was one of the first voices to publicly support homosexuality, and despite receiving tons of hate mail, she persevered.

NATIONAL COMING OUT DAY
OCTOBER 11th

National Coming Out Day was founded on October 11, 1988, marking the one-year anniversary of the 1987 March on Washington for Lesbian and Gay Rights. One of the founders of National Coming Out Day, Robert Eichsberg, reiterated the necessity of people coming out, claiming that most people find it easy to be homophobic because they assume they don't know anybody who identifies as queer. It's important to let people see members of the LGBTQ+ community, and reinforce that we are normal people who just happen to be LGBTQ+. Of course, many who live in states that deny protections to members of the LGBTQ+ community are forced to remain in the closet for their own safety.

the AIDS Crisis

1980s

The AIDS crisis spanned many years and defined the baby boomer generation, killing off millions of young men around the world—it was uncommon to be gay and *not* know a man dying of AIDS in the 1980s. The U.S. government moved extremely slowly in its response to this crisis, because it mostly affected gay men, blacks, Latinxs, and drug users.

AIDS Timeline (shortened):

June 5, 1981 Five gay men in Los Angeles are diagnosed with a rare lung infection. This is so out of the ordinary that the Centers for Disease Control publishes a report about it. Two of the men die by the time the report is published. This is the first known reporting of what is later known as AIDS, or acquired immunodeficiency syndrome, in which the body's immune system attacks itself, leaving those affected with little to no defense against any illness. The same day as the publication, a New York doctor calls the CDC to report that he has observed a formerly rare cancer—Kaposi's sarcoma—among gay men in New York. Calls flood in to the CDC of similar cases of mysterious weakened immune systems in gay men.

June 8, 1981 The CDC establishes a task force to identify the risk factors and define this mysterious disease.

July 3, 1981 After more deaths, the CDC releases another report, and the *New York Times* publishes an article about the rare "gay cancer." For the first time, the existence of this disease is made known to the general public.

August 11, 1981 Writer Larry Kramer holds a meeting of local gay men to try to garner monetary support for research. Only **$6,635** is raised, and that was the *entire* extent of AIDS funding for the year **1981**.

August 28, 1981 The CDC publishes a report showing that of the **108** reported cases, **94** percent of the patients are gay or bisexual, and **40** percent have died.

September 21, 1981 The first Kaposi's sarcoma clinic opens in San Francisco.

December 1981 A pediatric immunologist recognizes the symptoms of this mystery disease in five black infants whose mothers engaged in sex work. By the end of the year, there have been **337** reported cases of severe immunodeficiency, and **130** of those patients are already dead.

January 4, 1982 The first community-based AIDS service provider opens in New York City. Volunteers set up a hotline for information and counseling and are flooded with calls on their first night.

May 1982 San Francisco doctor Marcus Conant and activist Cleve Jones form Kaposi's Sarcoma Research and Education Foundation to provide information to gay men—the organization eventually becomes the San Francisco AIDS Foundation. The term "GRID" is used in a *New York Times* article: "gay-related immune deficiency." This increases the perception that AIDS is a gay disease.

June 27, 1982 A gay activist group creates a pamphlet on "safer sex" and distributes it at the International Lesbian & Gay Freedom Day Parade in San Francisco.

ONE AIDS DEATH EVERY 8 MINUTES

September 1982 CDC uses the term "AIDS" (acquired immunodeficiency syndrome) to define the disease. Two Democratic representatives introduce legislation for funding for AIDS research, but the resolution is not passed and Congress does not approve any AIDS funding until July **1983**.

January 1983 Ward **86**, the first outpatient AIDS clinic, opens in San Francisco.

March 1983 Larry Kramer publishes an essay called "**1,121** and Counting" in the *New York Native*. He begs for the community's support, condemning the government for its lack of support for sick and dying gay men.

May 1983 Richard Berkowitz and Michael Callen publish a booklet called *How to Have Sex in an Epidemic: One Approach*, which advocates the use of condoms.

May 1983 The Kaposi's Sarcoma Foundation sponsors the first AIDS candlelight vigils, in San Francisco and New York. This is the first time that people with AIDS have come together in public, and many photos of the event are taken and shared around the media—this is the first real publicity about the growing health epidemic. The *New York Times* publishes its first front-page story on AIDS. By the time it is published, **1,450** cases have been reported and **558** of those have already died.

June **1983** Eleven gay men issue a statement on the rights of people living with AIDS at the National AIDS Forum in Denver. They ask that people with AIDS be at the table when policies are made for them, that they be called "people with AIDS" instead of victims, and that they be treated with dignity. This eventually serves as the charter for the founding of the National Association of People with AIDS.

July **1983** The U.S. Public Health Service opens the National AIDS Hotline to answer the public's questions about the disease. The hotline is flooded with eight to ten thousand calls a day. San Francisco General Hospital opens the first inpatient AIDS ward, ward **5B**. It is at full capacity within days, and run by a compassionate, all-volunteer staff.

August **1983** Bobbi Campbell and his partner, Bobby Hilliard, appear on the cover of *Newsweek* for a story about AIDS. It is the first time that two gay men embracing are pictured on the cover of a national magazine. Bobbi dies of AIDS one year later, at age thirty-two.

September **1983** The CDC publishes a set of occupational exposure precautions for health care workers, as well as a study identifying all routes of HIV transmission, ruling out transmission by casual contact, food, water, or air. New York City physician Joseph Sonnabend, who has treated many men in New York, is threatened with eviction from his office for treating patients with AIDS. The state and Lambda Legal file the first AIDS discrimination lawsuit in response.

April **1984** The U.S. Department of Health and Human Services announces that it has found the cause of AIDS: a retrovirus called HTLV-III. The agency expresses hope that a vaccine will be developed within two years. As of **2019**, a vaccine has still not been developed.

March **1985** The U.S. Food and Drug Administration licenses a blood test to screen for HIV, and blood banks begin to screen their blood supply.

April **1985** Larry Kramer's play *The Normal Heart* opens. It covers the impact of the AIDS epidemic on the gay community and the growing rifts within the community. One month later, another play about gay people dealing with AIDS, William M. Hoffman's *As Is*, opens on Broadway.

July **1985** Actor Rock Hudson announces that he has AIDS. He is the first major celebrity to do so. He dies only three months later. In his will, he leaves **$250,000** to set up the American Foundation for AIDS Research.

August **1985** Ryan White, an Indiana teenager, is denied entry to his middle school. He contracted AIDS through blood banks. He speaks publicly on the need for AIDS education.

September **1985** Ronald Reagan mentions AIDS publicly and calls it a top priority. He denies that his administration's funding is inadequate.

October **1985** The U.S. Congress allocates **$190** million for AIDS research—**$70** million more than Reagan's budget request.

December **1985** After many bathhouses, bars, and clubs are closed in New York, the Los Angeles County Board of Supervisors tries to enact strict regulations against bathhouses to stop the spread of HIV. The bathhouse owners file suit and prove that their venues offer opportunities to provide HIV/AIDS education to the public. Later that month, the *Los Angeles Times* finds that the majority of Americans favor quarantining people with AIDS.

FRISKY CAN BE RISKY

January 1986 The CDC confirms that more people had been diagnosed with AIDS in 1985 than in all previous years—an 89 percent overall increase in AIDS cases. Of all AIDS cases from the previous years, over half of the patients have already died by this time. The CDC predicts twice as many new AIDS cases to come in 1986.

May 1986 The International Committee on the Taxonomy of Viruses names the virus that causes AIDS "human immunodeficiency virus," or HIV.

October 1986 The Robert Wood Johnson Foundation creates the *AIDS Health Services Program* in order to fund AIDS patient-care projects in eleven major cities, following the San Francisco Model of Care. The U.S. Health Resources and Services Administration begins its first AIDS health initiative to fund increased care in four major cities: New York, San Francisco, Los Angeles, and Miami. The CDC reports that AIDS disproportionately affects African Americans and Latinxs. The surgeon general also circulates a report that finally clarifies that HIV cannot be spread through casual contact, and that sex education, HIV testing, and the use of condoms can help prevent the spread of AIDS. A report is issued by the Institute of Medicine calling for a "massive media, educational, and public health campaign to curb the spread of HIV infection," and urges the need for a national commission on AIDS.

SAFE SEX

THE WAR FOR AIDS DRUGS

FREE ACCESSIBLE TREATMENTS

February 1987 AIDS activist Cleve Jones creates a panel for what will become the AIDS Memorial Quilt to honor a friend who has died of AIDS. The World Health Organization launches a program to raise awareness and come up with policies, as well as financial support to help those with HIV/AIDS. Famous pianist Liberace dies of AIDS.

March 1987 Larry Kramer founds ACT UP, the AIDS Coalition to Unleash Power (discussed more later). The Food and Drug Administration approves the first drug for AIDS, known as AZT. ACT UP stages its first protest, just after forming, in order to demand that the FDA immediately release the drug to anyone with AIDS at an affordable price.

April 1987 Princess Diana is photographed shaking the hand of an AIDS patient in a London hospital without wearing gloves or any protection. The photo is widely circulated and considered controversial in spite of the now widespread medical research showing that AIDS is not spread through casual contact.

May 1987 The U.S. Public Health Service adds HIV to its immigration exclusion list, mandating testing for any visa applicants. The HIV ban is not lifted until January 4, 2010. On May 31, six years after the epidemic starts, Ronald Reagan makes his first public speech about AIDS.

June 1987 Reagan creates the first presidential commission on AIDS.

ugust 1987 The FDA allows the first human esting of a possible vaccine against HIV; the results are not successful.

eptember 1987 The Centers for Disease Control aunch their first AIDS-related public service announcements at the end of the month, to kick off the start of AIDS Awareness Month in October. It reaches millions, and stresses that "everyone s at risk."

October 1987 The AIDS Memorial Quilt, with 1,920 four-by-eight-foot panels, goes on display for the first time in Washington, D.C. In a 94–2 Senate vote, the Helms Amendment requires federally financed AIDS education materials to promote abstinence only and bans any of the materials from mentioning homosexuality or drug use.

November 1987 The American Medical Association asserts that all doctors have an obligation to care for anyone with AIDS.

March 1988 Ryan White, the teenager who contracted AIDS in 1984 through a blood transfusion, testifies before the President's Commission on AIDS, describing the stigma he has endured. White's testimony helps shift public perception from AIDS as a gay-only problem to AIDS as an anyone problem. White will die of complications from the disease in 1990.

May 1988 The surgeon general launches a coordinated HIV/AIDS education campaign by mailing 107 million copies of a booklet called *Understanding AIDS* to all American households. It is the most widely distributed public health mailer in histo and also the first time that the federal governmen mentions sex in a public health campaign.

RUBBER UP FOR SAFETY

July 1988 The FDA announces that it will allo imports of a small amount of unapprove drugs for people with HIV/AIDS.

August 1988 David Purchase, a dru counselor, sets up the first needle-exchang program in the middle of a sidewalk i Tacoma, Washington. He purchases the needle out of pocket, and within five months exchange more than thirteen thousand clean needles fo contaminated needles. He later forms the Nort American Syringe Exchange Network.

October 1988 Over a thousand members o ACT UP engage in a sit-in to shut down the FDA' Maryland office, to protest the slow pace of th federal drug-approval process for drugs to trea HIV/AIDS. Eight days later, the FDA announce regulations to speed up the drug-approval proces

November 1988 Reagan signs the Health Omnibu Programs Extension Act into law, which authorize the use of federal funds for AIDS preventio education, and testing.

December 1988 World AIDS Day is observed for th first time.

1989 Congress creates the National Commissio on AIDS in September of this year. The U.S Health Resources and Services Administratio grants twenty million dollars for HIV care an treatment. The number of AIDS cases reache one hundred thousand.

1990 In July, Congress enacts th Americans with Disabilities Act, whic prohibits discrimination against peopl with disabilities—including HIV/AIDS. I August, months after Ryan White's deat

Congress enacts the Ryan White Comprehensive AIDS Resources Emergency Act to provide $**220.5** million in federal funding for community-based HIV care and treatment.

1991 Congress enacts the Housing Opportunities for People with AIDS Act, which provides grants for housing assistance to people with AIDS. In November, Magic Johnson announces that he is HIV-positive, and Freddie Mercury dies from AIDS that same month.

1992 AIDS becomes the number-one cause of death for American men ages twenty-five to forty-four. The FDA releases a diagnostic test that can be used to detect HIV in ten minutes.

1993 Congress enacts the National Institutes of Health Revitalization Act, which requires research agencies to include women and minorities in AIDS research. It also codifies the HIV immigration exclusion policy into law. The National Association of People with AIDS convenes the first "AIDS Watch" to lobby Congress for increased funding.

1994 AIDS becomes the leading cause of death for *all* Americans ages twenty-five to forty-four. The FDA approves an oral test for HIV. Pedro Zamora, a gay man with HIV, appears on *The Real World*, an MTV reality show. He dies shortly after it airs.

1995 The National Association of People with AIDS launches the first National HIV Testing Day. President Bill Clinton establishes his Presidential Advisory Council, and hosts the first White House conference on HIV/AIDS. The CDC concludes that syringe-exchange programs are an effective component of AIDS prevention strategy.

1996 For the first time since the beginning of the epidemic, the number of new AIDS cases diagnosed declines and AIDS is no longer the leading cause of death for all Americans. The AIDS Memorial Quilt is displayed, covering the entire National Mall in Washington, D.C. HIV/AIDS researcher David Ho advocates for a new strategy of HIV treatment, called "hit early, hit hard," which places patients on aggressive treatment regimens earlier in the course of their infection. The International AIDS Vaccine Initiative forms in order to speed the research for an HIV vaccine.

1997 The CDC reports that there is a substantial decline in AIDS deaths in the United States due to the use of "hit early, hit hard" highly active antiretroviral therapy (HAART). Clinton announces that finding an effective vaccine for HIV in the next ten years will be a top priority, and calls for the creation of an AIDS vaccine research center; the center is developed in **1999**.

1998 The CDC confirms that African Americans account for **49** percent of AIDS-related deaths, almost ten times the number of white deaths. The Congressional Black Caucus develops a call to action to request that the president and surgeon general declare HIV/AIDS a state of emergency in the African American community. Clinton declares AIDS a severe health crisis and launches initiatives to reduce the impact of HIV/AIDS on minorities. The government invests $**156** million in the Minority AIDS Initiative.

1999 The first National Black HIV/AIDS Awareness Day is launched to raise awareness about HIV/AIDS prevention, care, and treatment in communities of color.

2000 In response to the growing number of AIDS cases worldwide, a global crisis, Clinton announces the launch of the Millennium Vaccine Initiative to create incentives for developing vaccines against HIV, TB, and malaria.

2001 The first annual observance of HIV Vaccine Awareness Day occurs on May **18**. Generic drug manufacturers offer to produce discounted forms of HIV/AIDS drugs for developing countries.

2002 While the AIDS outbreak has slowed drastically within the gay community in the U.S., it is still a crisis in developing countries.

2003 The CDC calculates that around twenty-seven thousand of the forty thousand new infections in the U.S. result from transmission by individuals who do not know their status. The CDC publishes a new report, *Advancing HIV Prevention*, to reduce barriers for early diagnosis.

2004 The FDA approves the use of a rapid HIV test kit that works with oral fluid samples to provide accurate in-home results in twenty minutes, eliminating the need for a visit to a clinic to get a test.

2006 The CDC releases revised HIV testing recommendations, advocating for all adults aged thirteen to sixty-four to be tested yearly.

2007 The CDC launches a social media campaign, *Prevention IS Care*, for health care providers who deliver care to those with HIV. Since **1981**, the CDC reports that over **565,000** people have died of AIDS in the U.S.

2008 President George W. Bush reauthorizes a bill that contains a rider lifting the blanket ban on HIV-positive travelers to the United States on a case-by-case basis, giving the U.S. Department of Health and Human Services the authority to admit selected individuals with HIV/AIDS into the United States. The first National Gay Men's HIV/AIDS Awareness Day is recognized on September **27**.

2009 President Barack Obama calls for the development of a National HIV/AIDS Strategy for the United States. Obama announces that the U.S. will universally lift the HIV travel and immigration ban in January **2010**. Obama also signs the Consolidated Appropriations Act to modify the ban on the use of federal funds for needle exchanges.

2010 President Obama signs the Patient Protection and Affordable Care Act, which gives access to care to all Americans and offers special protections for those with chronic illnesses like HIV/AIDS. At the Eighteenth International AIDS Conference, the National Institutes of Health show that a daily dose of HIV drugs reduces the risk of infection for HIV-negative men who have sex with other men, suggesting that the use of a pre-exposure drug would be beneficial in target populations.

2011 Secretary of State Hillary Clinton shares a vision of creating an AIDS-free generation. Obama announces efforts to increase the availability of treatment to those with HIV/AIDS.

2012 The FDA approves the first at-home HIV test, and approves the use of the drug Truvada, a pre-exposure prophylaxis (PrEP) for adults who do not have HIV but are at risk. This drug reduces the risk of getting the virus through sexual activity. The AIDS Memorial Quilt is displayed in Washington, D.C., for the first time since **1996**.

2013 The National Minority AIDS Council releases an action plan to mitigate the impact of HIV on black gay and bisexual men. South African anti-apartheid leader, political prisoner, and South African president Nelson Mandela dies. After his presidency, he spent the rest of his career working to address the AIDS epidemic in South Africa.

2014 Due to the Affordable Care Act, insurance companies are barred from discriminating against customers with preexisting conditions and cannot impose an annual coverage limit. Douglas Brooks is appointed as the director of the White House Office of National AIDS policy—the first African American HIV-positive person to hold the position. The FDA announces that it will change the blood donor guideline for gay men from a permanent deferral to one year since their last sexual contact.

2015 After Governor Mike Pence resists needle exchanges, Indiana announces an HIV outbreak due to injection drug use. By the end of the year, **184** new cases of HIV are linked to this outbreak. Researchers find that antiretroviral therapy is effective at preventing sexual transmission of HIV from an HIV-positive partner to an uninfected partner. The CDC reports that HIV diagnoses fell by **19** percent annually between **2005** and **2014**. There were large declines in infection rates for African Americans, needle users, and heterosexuals, but infections of gay and bisexual men did not decrease so drastically.

2016 Researchers report that a man taking Truvada, the HIV-prevention pill, has contracted HIV. This is the first case of infection in someone taking the PrEP drug. The UN holds its **2016** High-Level Meeting on Ending AIDS, but more than fifty nations block the participation of groups representing LGBTQ+ people. The final resolution hardly mentions those at highest risk for contracting HIV/AIDS: gay men, sex workers, trans people, and drug users.

2017 The Bill and Melinda Gates Foundation invests $**140** million in an HIV-prevention tool that delivers HIV prevention continuously, eliminating the need for a daily PrEP. The Muslim American organization RAHMA launches the first Faith HIV/AIDS Awareness Day to rally U.S. faith communities to raise awareness of HIV/AIDS in their congregations and take a stand against stigma.

2018 A Northwestern University study, "Keep It Up!," an online HIV-prevention program that targets young men who have sex with men, is found to reduce sexually transmitted infections by **40** percent. The program offers video clips and interactive games and is the first of its kind.

2019 At the Conference on Retroviruses and Opportunistic Infections, researchers announce that a person with HIV has been cured: the patient has no detectable HIV three years after a bone marrow transplant from a donor. This type of treatment is dangerous and costly, but helps prove that HIV can be cured.

Public Perception

Unfortunately, homophobia, social stigma, and AIDS go hand in hand. As this disease spread rapidly, the communities it affected were largely *already* marginalized. Gay men, intravenous drug users, sex workers, African Americans, and Latinxs were most affected. All of this wrapped up into what is known as AIDS-related stigma. Firstly, people feared the disease. To the uneducated public, AIDS was synonymous with death, and how it spread was the subject of speculation—some *New York Times* articles claimed it was spread through saliva or social contact, a myth the CDC went on to debunk. AIDS patients literally wasted away, creating a physically gaunt appearance. The perception of AIDS as a "gay disease"—even now, in 2019, despite the fact that currently the most common AIDS patient is an intravenous drug user—coincides with the prevalence of homophobia. Racism, sexism, and other forms of discrimination *have* been publicly condemned (not that this means they don't exist! Discrimination is still rife within any marginalized community) by way of laws, general social conduct, and so on. People can be held more accountable for their discrimination toward these protected communities, but the LGBTQ+ population remains an open target, as there has never been a cultural consensus on whether homophobia is okay or not. Because AIDS was seen as a "gay disease," there was no urgency in the government's response and funding. There was little urgency or outrage by those outside the gay community. Even today, as anti-discrimination laws are still not federal mandate, plenty of states allow people to discriminate against someone on the basis of sexual orientation or gender identity—meaning that loss of jobs, homelessness, lack of health insurance, and so on keep our community at risk. Members of the LGBTQ+ community often have to seek out sex work to meet basic needs. Doctors can discriminate against LGBTQ+ people and refuse to treat them. Stigma leads to sickness and sickness leads to death.

Government Response

The government response to the AIDS crisis has been widely criticized. The Reagan administration was slow to respond. Early in his presidency, Reagan cut budgets at the CDC, and the social conservatives who had voted for him were not interested in helping fund research for a disease that was associated with homosexuality. Medical research and prevention campaigns were stifled by the scant funding. It was not until six years after AIDS had taken hold in the gay community that the administration took steps to raise AIDS awareness. The first drug to treat AIDS, AZT, became available in 1987, and Congress allocated thirty million dollars to help states purchase AIDS drugs. However, the prescription price rose and rose until it was out of reach for most. The CDC wrote grants for gay men's health educators who had pro-sex approaches (such as safe sex pamphlets); however, social conservatives were so offended by this that they demanded legislation, the Helms Amendment, to require any federally funded sex education program to promote abstinence. This amendment, and the not-so-covert homophobia behind it, likely caused more members of our community to contract the disease and die. In 2010, Barack Obama created a National HIV/AIDS Strategy that called attention to gay and bisexual men and transgender women; he also signed the Affordable Care Act, which prohibited insurance companies from denying health care to anyone with a pre-existing condition, including HIV.

RESPONSE WITHIN THE COMMUNITY

Though the government has been unresponsive and obstructive at times, the gay community itself mobilized. Some members focused on prevention: condom awareness campaigns, AIDS trading cards, and so on. Others focused on lobbying for policy changes and government response. Activists formed groups, most notably ACT UP.

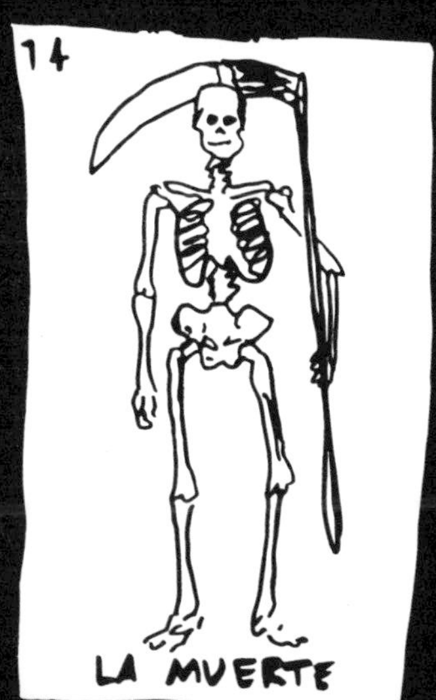

AIDS MEMORIAL QUILT

1987

Established in 1987, the AIDS Memorial Quilt is a giant, beautiful quilt made to celebrate the lives of people who died of AIDS. The quilt is the largest piece of community folk art in the world. It was initially thought up by Cleve Jones because at the time, many people who died of AIDS did not receive a proper funeral. There was a harsh social stigma around homosexuality, and the AIDS crisis heightened it. Often, funeral homes would refuse to hold services for AIDS victims, saying they were unable to handle their infected remains. Thus, the AIDS Memorial Quilt gave people an opportunity to celebrate their loved ones. Each panel is approximately the size of an adult grave, and commemorates one victim. The quilt is still maintained, and panels are added year by year. The AIDS Memorial Quilt, when shown on the Mall in Washington, brought to light how huge the AIDS pandemic really was, and increased awareness of the need to fund AIDS service organizations.

ACT UP

1987

With the lack of government response, gay communities had to form their own groups to fight AIDS. ACT UP—AIDS Coalition to Unleash Power—was founded in New York in 1987 by Larry Kramer and a group of other advocates with the goal to raise awareness of the AIDS epidemic and thereby help end it. ACT UP organized many protests to draw attention to the cause. They demonstrated on Wall Street numerous times, demanding access to AIDS drugs and protesting the sky-high price of AZT, the only federally approved AIDS drug on the market. At the post office, ACT UP protested once again, and the now infamous Silence = Death poster was displayed, which urged people to not keep quiet. The poster featured a pink triangle—a nod to the Nazi symbol used to identify homosexual prisoners. This particular protest drew a lot of media attention, as the media often already filmed at the post office in stories of last-minute tax filers. ACT UP's largest demonstration was in October 1988, when they shut down the Food and Drug Administration for a day: they blocked doors, walkways, and the road as they chanted, "Hey, hey, FDA, how many people have you killed today?" Police arrested hundreds. ACT UP participated in many other rallies and functioned as a largely anarchistic group, but was arguably the most effective health activist group by pressuring companies and government agencies.

NO BED! NOW I'M DEAD

ACT UP LOS ANGELES

Something BAD is brewing for November

EDUCATE!

¡EDUQUE!

AND THE BAND PLAYED ON

1987

And the Band Played On, by journalist Randy Shilts, was an investigative look at the AIDS crisis, in which he heavily criticized the government's response. He claimed that although the disease was indeed caused by sexual contact, the fact that the government was slow and apathetic to respond allowed AIDS to spread rapidly and decimate the gay male population. Shilts chose to write the book because he himself was a gay man—he saw the crisis being portrayed in the media as a joke, because people felt safe to assume that if they didn't know any gay people, this crisis couldn't affect them. It was another way of "othering" the community. He described the desperate action of those in the gay community to gain public awareness and preventive education, and how they were often ignored. He criticized the Centers for Disease Control for their lackadaisical response to a large-scale crisis, and the Reagan administration for claiming AIDS was a priority, yet not dedicating any extra funding to it. He criticized the media for first ignoring the crisis, then only reporting information when the crisis affected heterosexuals, like people who received blood transfusions; he also blamed the media for hyping the means of transmission and prompting a homophobic response by claiming that AIDS could be contracted by any contact. The book was an award-winning success, but Shilts was disappointed that it did not prompt any radical response to the AIDS crisis.

KEITH HARING

MAY 4, 1958–FEBRUARY 16, 1990

Keith Haring grew up in Pennsylvania and moved to New York City to attend the School of Visual Arts, where he quickly found his place in a thriving and growing art community. When he began to notice blacked-out, unused ad panels in the subway stations (thanks, MTA!), he started filling them with large chalk line drawings. Recognition for his innovative and unique style grew, and he began to show his work in solo and group exhibitions around New York City. He opened the Pop Shop in 1986, where he sold his artwork on T-shirts, buttons, and other trinkets. This prompted some criticism from the elitist art world, but Haring strongly felt that he should allow everyday people access to his artwork. Haring is known not only for his bold style, but for his social messaging, which he projected across dozens of murals and public artworks. One of his most iconic, *Crack Is Wack*, created in 1986 amid the crack epidemic in New York City, was initially drawn on an abandoned handball court in Harlem. Haring used his voice to make powerful social statements about the state of the community and the lack of response from city officials—his handball wall faced the highway and acted almost like a billboard. Haring was not given permission to do this, and was arrested for graffiti. At the height of his skyrocketing career in the eighties, Haring was diagnosed with AIDS; he died of AIDS-related complications in 1990. Although his career was short-lived, he is arguably one of the most famous street artists, and worked hard to make his art accessible to all and to use his voice to address social issues.

Madonna

AUGUST 16, 1958–PRESENT

Since the beginning of her career, Madonna, one of the biggest superstar-diva gay icons of our time, has been one of the best allies the LGBTQ+ community has ever seen. You may know her through hits such as "Like a Virgin" and "Papa Don't Preach," but outside of her classic, decade-defining music, Madonna was and still is a true queer-ally warrior. With decades of AIDS activism under her belt and open support for the LGBTQ+ community, Madonna has helped shape the landscape of a better world for queers everywhere through her activism and her music. I mean, come on! She helped introduce voguing to mainstream America *and* publicly boos homophobia any chance she has. Her support throughout her career has helped bring acceptance and visibility to issues surrounding the LGBTQ+ community.

FANTASIA FAIR PARIS IS BURNING BINET USA TRANSGENDER SYMBOL LESLIE FEINBERG BRANDON TEENA AIDS TRADING CARDS ONE ARCHIVES DON'T ASK, DON'T TELL DEFENSE OF MARRIAGE ACT ELLEN DEGENERES THE WALT WHITMAN COMMUNITY SCHOOL THE AL-FATIHA FOUNDATION MATTHEW SHEPARD

FANTASIA FAIR

1990s

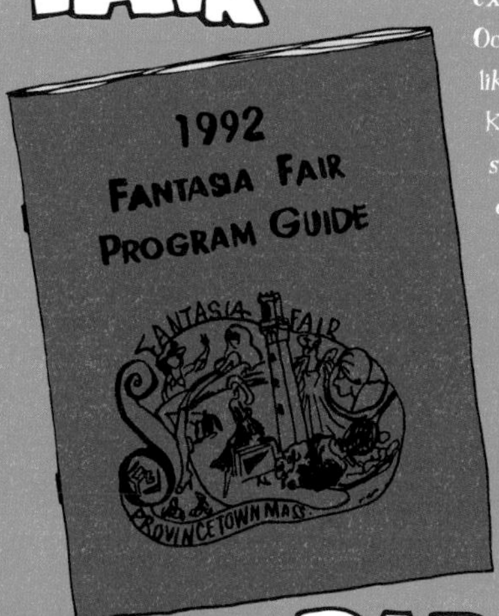

1992
FANTASIA FAIR
PROGRAM GUIDE
FANTASIA FAIR
PROVINCETOWN MASS.

Founded in 1975, the Fantasia Fair is a weeklong event for transgender, questioning, and genderqueer people to present and explore their gender in a safe and affirming space. Held every October in Provincetown, Massachusetts, the fair boasts events like fashion shows, talent shows, workshops, and banquets. Ariadne Kane and other members of Boston's Cherrystone support group started Fantasia Fair in response to the need for a safe space for cross-dressers and transgender people to learn about themselves. When it first started out, Fantasia Fair was geared toward the cross-dressing community. However, in the 1990s, the fair began to attract a more diverse audience that included trans women, trans men, and genderqueer people. After tweaking the fair schedule and events, Fantasia Fair essentially became what it is today: a transgender convention spread around the town, offering workshops on topics like gender change and identity, makeup and clothing, relationships, and other topics relating to gender.

PARIS IS BURNING

1990

Paris Is Burning, a 1990 documentary by Jennie Livingston, followed the drag ball culture of New York City and the intersections of the black, Latinx, gay, and transgender communities within the culture. Livingston, a lesbian filmmaker, was inspired to make the documentary after meeting two young men voguing (striking a pose . . . while dancing)—something she'd never seen before. She then began attending balls and meeting performers like Venus Xtravaganza, Octavia St. Laurent, and Dorian Corey. After Livingston created a trailer, the production received enough funding from grants to finish the documentary. The film documented the extravagant ball competitions (much like the ones seen in *Pose*, see page 124) as well as interviews with members of the scene—their stories, and how they found their "house." If you haven't seen *Pose* (yet, because you must), you might not understand that a "house" is a home for queer youth who faced rejection from their biological families due to their sexual orientation or gender identity. As its subjects were members of the LGBTQ+ community, they were no strangers to issues within the community, such as AIDS, racism, poverty, homophobia, and homelessness. The film touches on all of these.

BiNet USA

1990

BiNet USA was the first national bisexuality organization in the United States. Its goal was to promote bisexual visibility and maintain a strong community. It has been involved in a number of policy initiatives and campaigns, and was the force behind Celebrate Bisexuality Day, which evolved into Bisexual Awareness Week in 2014. The organization was conceived to combat the marginalization and erasure of bisexual people by some in both the straight and LGBTQ+ communities. Campaigns such as this one are highly important, as they create visibility for others questioning their sexuality, and allow the members of the community to feel less marginalized.

Transgender Symbol

1993

The symbol that is used to represent transgender people was designed in 1993 by trans woman Holly Boswell. The symbol is a combination of the female, male, and hermaphroditic gender symbols. Holly was a trans activist and spent most of her life learning and growing with a close community of trans and queer people. She was based in Asheville, North Carolina, and with Jessica Britton cofounded the city's Phoenix Transgender Support Group in 1986—a queer, trans, and gender-nonconforming support group that is still around today.

Leslie Feinberg

SEPTEMBER 1, 1949–NOVEMBER 15, 2014

Leslie Feinberg, transgender warrior, played a significant role in creating and cultivating the trans and nonbinary culture that we are living in today. Using the pronouns "ze" and "hir," Leslie spent hir life fighting for trans rights up until the very end, practicing activism as part of hir everyday routine. In 1993, ze published *Stone Butch Blues*, a novel "written by an author who has lived the non-fiction" of it all, providing a work of literature that gives insight into living as transgender in the nineties.

Brandon Teena

1993

Brandon Teena was a trans man who was murdered in Humboldt, Nebraska, in 1993, and is the subject of the film *Boys Don't Cry*. As a child, he felt different and often bound his chest to pass as a boy, then began dating girls. He began a relationship with a girl, and attempted to make enough money for them to live together. However, when Brandon's mother found out about the relationship, she sent him for a psychiatric evaluation. Eventually, Brandon moved away from home to another town in Nebraska, where he started a new life identifying as a man. He began dating a girl named Lana Tisdel and made friends with his future murderers, John L. Lotter and Thomas Nissen. After forging checks, Brandon was arrested—his girlfriend bailed him out but realized he had been held in the female section of the jail, and he was outed as transgender. It is unclear if Tisdel maintained the relationship after his outing (in the movie, she does, but she disputed this after the movie came out and was given an undisclosed sum of money in settlement). Shortly after this, word spread that Brandon was transgender. At a Christmas party, Lotter and Nissen exposed Brandon by pulling down his pants and "proving" that he was a woman because he had a vagina. They then raped him and threatened to kill him if he told anybody about the rape. Brandon went to the emergency room and was administered a rape kit, but it was lost. Somehow, the two men found out about Brandon's report of the rape and went to find him, locating him in the house of his friend Lisa Lambert. They forced their way in, and shot and killed Tisdel's sister's boyfriend, Phillip DeVine, and Lisa. They then found Brandon hiding under the bed, shot him, and stabbed him to "make sure" he was dead. Nissen was sentenced to life in prison, and Lotter was given the death penalty. As if Brandon hadn't suffered enough, news outlets consistently referred to him as a lesbian because he hadn't had gender reassignment surgery, and his mother publicly objected to the use of the pronoun "he" and inscribed his grave with DAUGHTER, SISTER, & FRIEND.

AIDS Trading Cards

1993

When you think of trading cards, your mind probably automatically goes to baseball cards, Pokémon cards, I don't know, maybe even Yu-Gi-Oh! But in 1993, comic book publisher Eclipse came out with a new type of deck. In the midst of the AIDS crisis, the AIDS Awareness trading deck served as an easy and accessible way to learn about HIV/AIDS, how to prevent it, famous and notable people who had contracted it, and other information about the topic, all while making learning not so boring with the magic of a deck of trading cards. The full deck totaled 110 illustrated and information-packed cards.

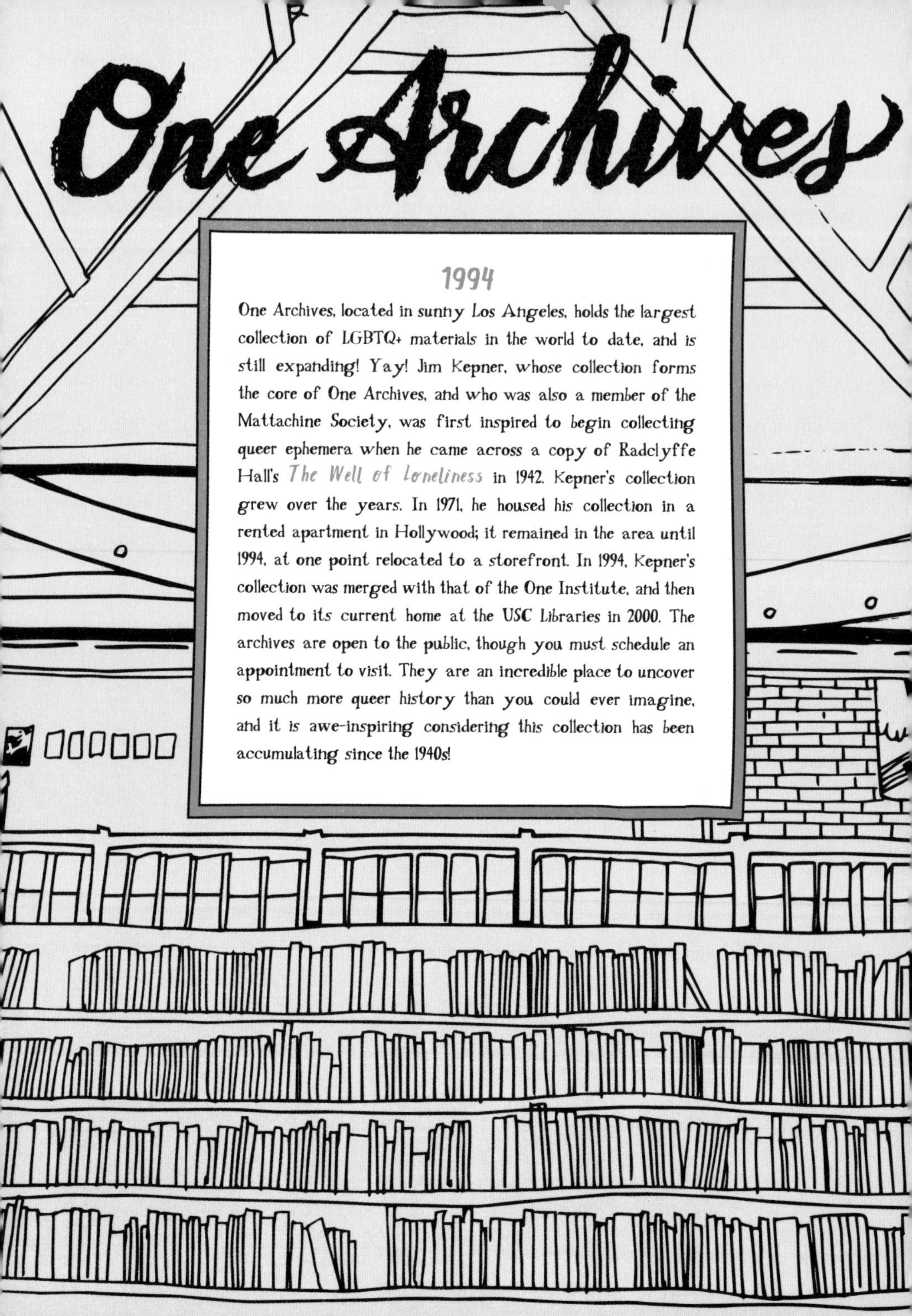

One Archives

1994

One Archives, located in sunny Los Angeles, holds the largest collection of LGBTQ+ materials in the world to date, and is still expanding! Yay! Jim Kepner, whose collection forms the core of One Archives, and who was also a member of the Mattachine Society, was first inspired to begin collecting queer ephemera when he came across a copy of Radclyffe Hall's *The Well of Loneliness* in 1942. Kepner's collection grew over the years. In 1971, he housed his collection in a rented apartment in Hollywood; it remained in the area until 1994, at one point relocated to a storefront. In 1994, Kepner's collection was merged with that of the One Institute, and then moved to its current home at the USC Libraries in 2000. The archives are open to the public, though you must schedule an appointment to visit. They are an incredible place to uncover so much more queer history than you could ever imagine, and it is awe-inspiring considering this collection has been accumulating since the 1940s!

Don't Ask, Don't Tell

1994

Don't Ask, Don't Tell was the U.S. military policy instituted by Bill Clinton that lasted until 2011. This policy ever-so-kindly prohibited military people from discriminating against closeted homosexuals while not allowing openly gay individuals to join the military. So basically, you could be gay in the military, as long as you didn't tell anybody about it. Like, you can go ahead and be gay all you want, just don't bother anyone. While it sounds horrific now, this policy was actually a pretty serious relaxation of restrictions that had previously been in place for LGBTQ+ military members. Before this policy, LGBTQ+ people were not even allowed to join the military—in fact, it was alleged that the presence of fabulous LGBTQ+ people would "create an unacceptable risk to the high standards of morale, good order and discipline, and unit cohesion." Not cool. Eventually, legislation to repeal Don't Ask, Don't Tell was enacted, and in 2011 a federal court barred the policy. Don't Ask, Don't Tell officially ended on September 20, 2011, and gays were allowed to be out and proud in the military!

Defense of Marriage Act

AKA DOMA

1996

This *very* rude law was passed on September 21, 1996. It defined marriage as an institution existing solely between a man and a woman, which enabled states to refuse to recognize same-sex marriages that had previously been recognized under the law of other states. Not cool. This law was a big deal because it barred same-sex spouses from receiving federal marriage benefits, like insurance, social security, citizenship, financial aid, and so on. It was not overturned by the Supreme Court until 2013.

Ellen DeGeneres

JANUARY 26, 1958–PRESENT

Ellen DeGeneres is an openly gay comedian and TV personality who hosts her own award-winning talk show, *The Ellen DeGeneres Show*. She is one of the best-known members of the LGBTQ+ community and is a huge advocate for LGBTQ+ rights. Ellen was not always out as a gay woman—she came out to the public in an interview with Oprah Winfrey in 1997, and soon after, her character Ellen Morgan on her TV sitcom, *Ellen*, came out as a lesbian. At that time, it was a very controversial and risky career move. Soon after she came out, Ellen's show was canceled. As time passed, people began to embrace Ellen as the amazing lesbian comedian she is, and now Ellen is a hero among the queer community. Aside from supporting multiple LGBTQ+ charities and foundations, she also is a big animal rights activist. Fun fact: Ellen wanted to be a veterinarian growing up! She is married to actress Portia de Rossi, and they are an adorable lesbian power couple!

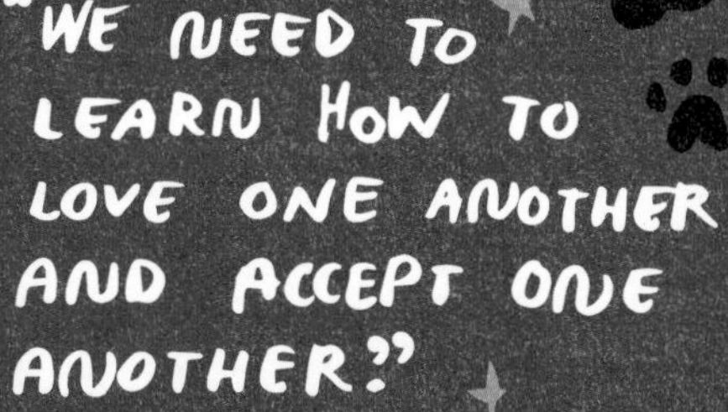

"WE NEED TO LEARN HOW TO LOVE ONE ANOTHER AND ACCEPT ONE ANOTHER."

the Walt Whitman Community School

1997

The Walt Whitman Community School was founded in Dallas, Texas, and was the first LGBTQ+ private school in the United States. It was cofounded by two teachers who had worked together at another school where anti-LGBTQ+ sentiments were often thrown around. The school had nine students in its first year, and was unaccredited. The school provided financial assistance to its students, and fund-raised in the community, but it struggled financially and never met its small enrollment goal of thirty students. The school abruptly closed right before the 2004 school year. Although it did not last, it was the only LGBTQ+ private school outside Manhattan or Los Angeles, and was notable in a conservative state.

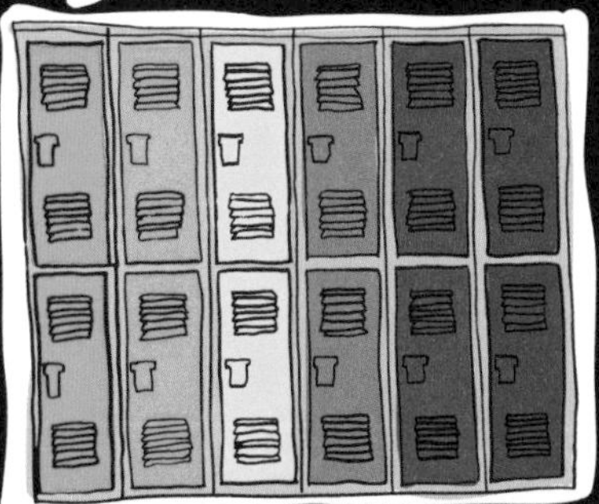

the Al-Fatiha Foundation

1997

The Al-Fatiha Foundation was a pro-LGBTQ+ Muslim organization in operation from 1997 to 2011. Founded by Pakistani American Faisal Alam, this organization worked to combat homophobia in Muslim communities and promoted progressive beliefs on equality, justice, and peace, providing support to individuals struggling with sexual orientation or identity in relation to Islam. What began as an online community quickly turned into live chapters throughout the United States and several other countries, where people would gather to discuss these topics in person. The foundation was, unfortunately, very short-lived, partially due to the unforgiving condemnation of the jihadist group Al-Muhajiroun, which claimed that supporting queers is equivalent to abandoning Islam.

Matthew Shepard

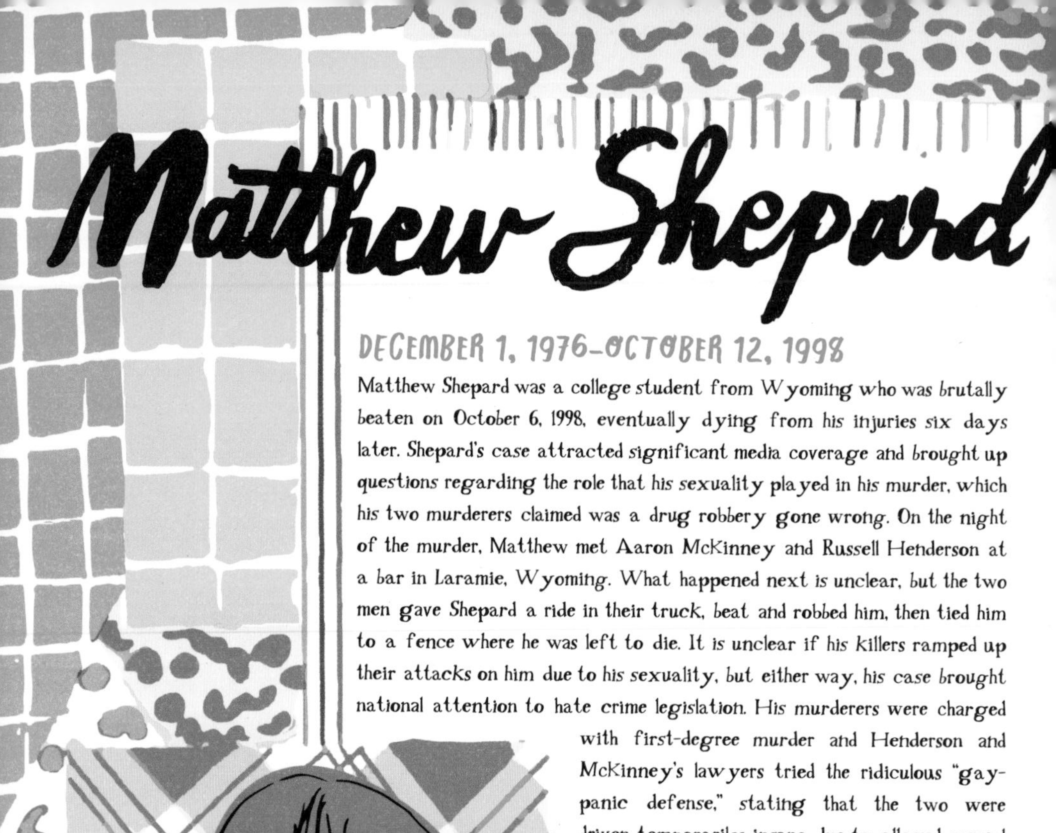

DECEMBER 1, 1976–OCTOBER 12, 1998

Matthew Shepard was a college student from Wyoming who was brutally beaten on October 6, 1998, eventually dying from his injuries six days later. Shepard's case attracted significant media coverage and brought up questions regarding the role that his sexuality played in his murder, which his two murderers claimed was a drug robbery gone wrong. On the night of the murder, Matthew met Aaron McKinney and Russell Henderson at a bar in Laramie, Wyoming. What happened next is unclear, but the two men gave Shepard a ride in their truck, beat and robbed him, then tied him to a fence where he was left to die. It is unclear if his killers ramped up their attacks on him due to his sexuality, but either way, his case brought national attention to hate crime legislation. His murderers were charged with first-degree murder and Henderson and McKinney's lawyers tried the ridiculous "gay-panic defense," stating that the two were driven temporarily insane due to alleged sexual advances. Under U.S. federal law and Wyoming state law at the time, crimes committed due to sexual orientation could *not* be prosecuted as hate crimes; this fact motivated many in the media to ramp up their attempts to extend hate crime legislation. In 2007, the Matthew Shepard Act made it through Congress with bipartisan votes, but George W. Bush stated that he would veto the legislation and eventually the bill was dropped. In 2009, the Matthew Shepard and James Byrd Jr. Hate Crimes Prevention Act again made it to Congress, and this time it was signed into law by Barack Obama. This bill expands the federal hate crime law to include crimes that are related to a victim's actual or perceived gender, sexual orientation, or disability.

2000s

QUEER EYE FOR THE STRAIGHT GUY TEGAN & SARA FIRST LEGAL SAME-SEX MARRIAGE THE L WORD PROPOSITION 8 ALISON BECHDEL JAZZ JENNINGS RUPAUL'S DRAG RACE

Queer Eye

2003

Queer Eye for the Straight Guy was a reality TV show that aired on Bravo from 2003 to 2007. It basically had gay men fulfilling the stereotypes of being more fashionable, better groomed, and just generally more aware than their straight counterparts, and giving straight guys makeovers to improve their lives. While these seem like tokenizing stereotypes, at the time it was groundbreaking to even air a show starring gay men. The start of the new millennium was not only a new beginning, but also an invitation for more LGBTQ+ content to be broadcast into the homes of millions. Ellen DeGeneres's coming out during the late nineties helped pave the way for shows like the gay-centric *Queer Eye*. The show ran for five successful seasons, and its title was shortened to just *Queer Eye* during its third season to include people of other sexual orientations. The Fab Five cast included Ted Allen, Food; Kyan Douglas, Grooming; Thom Filicia, Design; Carson Kressley, Fashion; and Jai Rodriguez, Culture. After the first couple of seasons, the creators decided to do a spinoff, *Queer Eye for the Straight Girl*, which did not have the same success as the original and was canceled after one season.

Tegan & Sara

2000s

Tegan and Sara are identical twin sisters from Canada, both of whom are lesbians. They formed their namesake band in 1998 and built a broad fan base over the next two decades with their genre-bending series of albums, each significantly different from the last in style and presentation. The queer duo have contributed to making the LGBTQ+ community more visible in the music world.

FIRST LEGAL SAME-SEX MARRIAGE

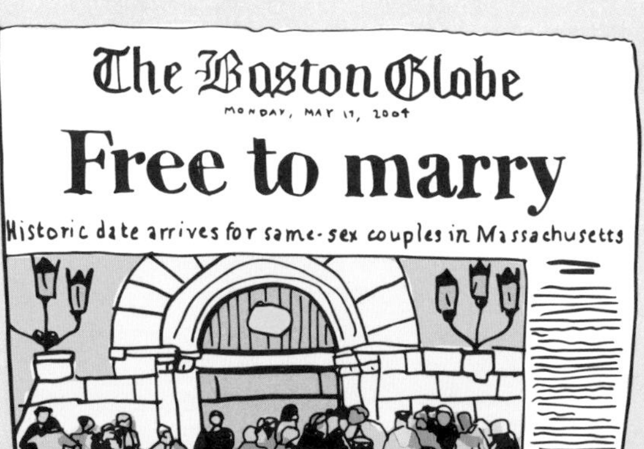
The Boston Globe
MONDAY, MAY 17, 2004
Free to marry
Historic date arrives for same-sex couples in Massachusetts

2004

On April 11, 2001, GLAD (Gay and Lesbian Advocates and Defenders, not to be confused with GLAAD) sued the Massachusetts Department of Health in the state's superior court on behalf of seven queer couples who had been turned down for obtaining marriage licenses earlier that year. They argued that it was unconstitutional under Massachusetts law for same-sex couples to be excluded from being able to marry legally. The case advanced to the Massachusetts Supreme Judicial Court in 2003, where the defendants argued that since marriage was historically based on procreation duties between two members of the opposite sex, same-sex couples did not fit the bill of what marriage was intended for, since queer couples can't pop out babies as fast and as efficiently as straight couples can. LOL. Lucky for us, the court ruled 4–3 in favor of allowing same-sex marriage! They officially concluded that the state "may not deny the protections, benefits, and obligations conferred by civil marriage to two individuals of the same sex who wish to marry" and also forbade the "creation of second-class citizens." The court gave the state legislature 180 days to come up with any argument in rebuttal to the court's wishes; the legislature failed to do so. So basically, queers in Massachusetts were the first queers in the United States to full on, 100 percent, all the way get married, receiving all the same recognitions and benefits as straight married people do! Woo! And now for the part you've been waiting for . . . On May 17, 2004, Tanya McCloskey and Marcia Kadish were declared wife and wife, becoming the first legally married same-sex couple in the United States. Almost twenty-five hundred same-sex couples applied for marriage licenses in Massachusetts in the first week. Such history, such love!

the L Word

2004

The L Word was a TV series that closely followed the lives of a tight-knit group of lesbians living in Los Angeles in the mid-2000s. The main crew includes Bette, Tina, Shane, Alice, Dana, Jenny, Helena, and Kit, who weave their way in and out of friendships and love affairs over the six seasons of the show's run. *The L Word* was a landmark for gay representation in Hollywood, as the main story line is essentially that of mostly nonstraight women and their ventures into the realms of love and lust. Created by Ilene Chaiken, Michele Abbott, and Kathy Greenberg, ***The L Word*** was a success in providing lesbians everywhere some quality content to binge-watch, even years after its final episode in 2009—although more than ten years later, the show was rebooted with many of the same characters plus some, under the reunion name of ***The L Word: Generation Q***. The original series is sometimes referred to as a rite of passage when coming out as a lesbian, although there is some content that is quite outdated, like subtle hostilities toward trans characters in later seasons.

Proposition 8

2008

PROP 8 SUCKS

Proposition 8 was an *extremely rude* ballot proposition in California that declared that same-sex couples could not marry! Before this proposition, there was another proposition in California (warning: we use the word "proposition" a lot in this entry. Like, a lot more than we've ever used it before) called Proposition 22, which maintained that only marriages between a man and a woman were valid and recognized in California. Proposition 22 was struck down in 2008 as well, but shortly before it was struck down, Proposition 8 made it onto the ballot in order to maintain the sanctity of marriage (or whatever gay-marriage naysayers say). In a notoriously liberal state, voters approved the ballot measure. However, almost immediately after the proposition was voted on, lawsuits were filed seeking to eliminate the proposition, claiming that it was unconstitutional. In 2010, a federal judge agreed and struck down Proposition 8. Take that, haters!

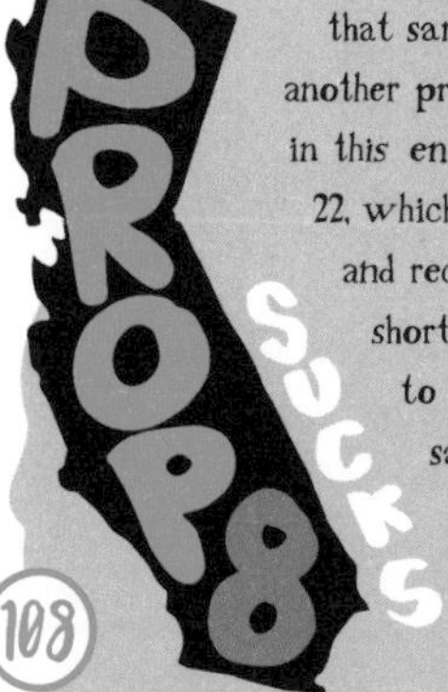

Alison Bechdel

SEPTEMBER 10, 1960–PRESENT

Alison Bechdel is a dope dyke cartoonist who created the long-running comic strip *Dykes to Watch Out For*, one of the earliest mainstream representations of lesbians, which ran from 1983 to 2008. In 1985, her comic strip introduced the Bechdel test, which measures the representation of women in fiction. A piece of fiction passes the Bechdel test if it includes at least two women who have a conversation about something other than a man. In 2006, Bechdel published her graphic memoir *Fun Home*, which brought her huge commercial success—with good reason. Alison, if you are reading this, *Fun Home* is my (Chess's) favorite book ever and it means so much to me!!! *Fun Home* was adapted as a musical and subsequently won five Tony awards in 2015.

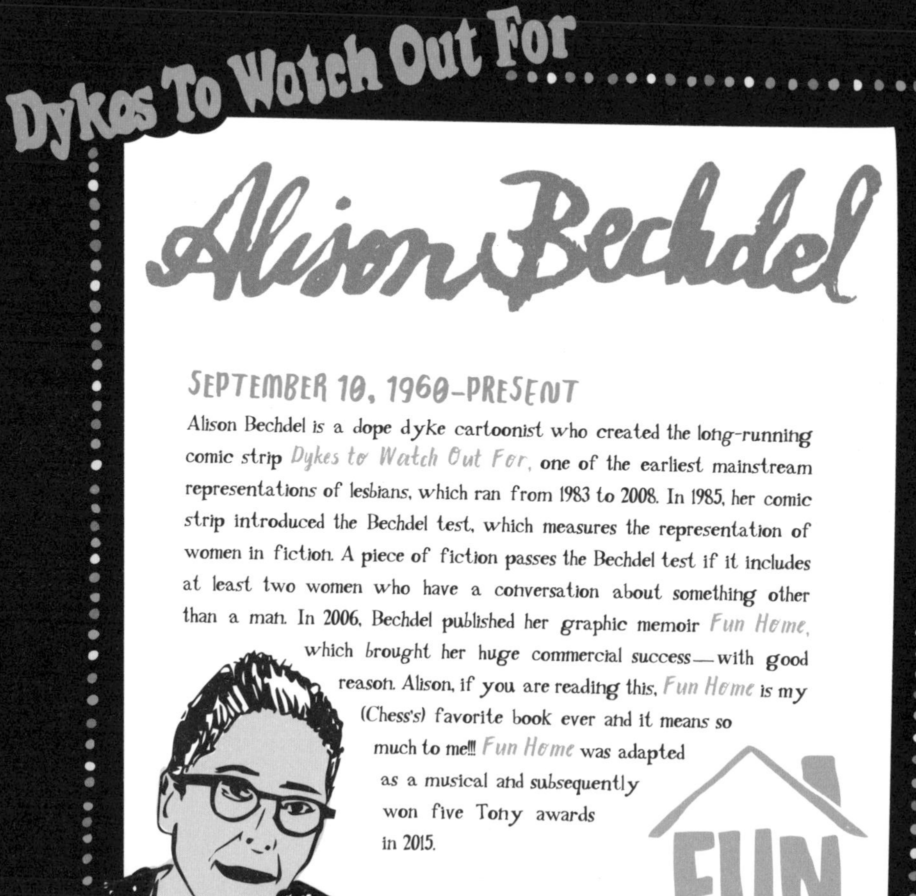

FUN HOME
THE BECHDEL TEST
I ONLY GO TO A MOVIE IF IT SATISFIES THREE BASIC REQUIREMENTS. ONE, IT HAS TO HAVE AT LEAST TWO WOMEN IN IT..
..WHO, TWO, TALK TO EACH OTHER ABOUT, THREE, SOMETHING BESIDES A MAN.

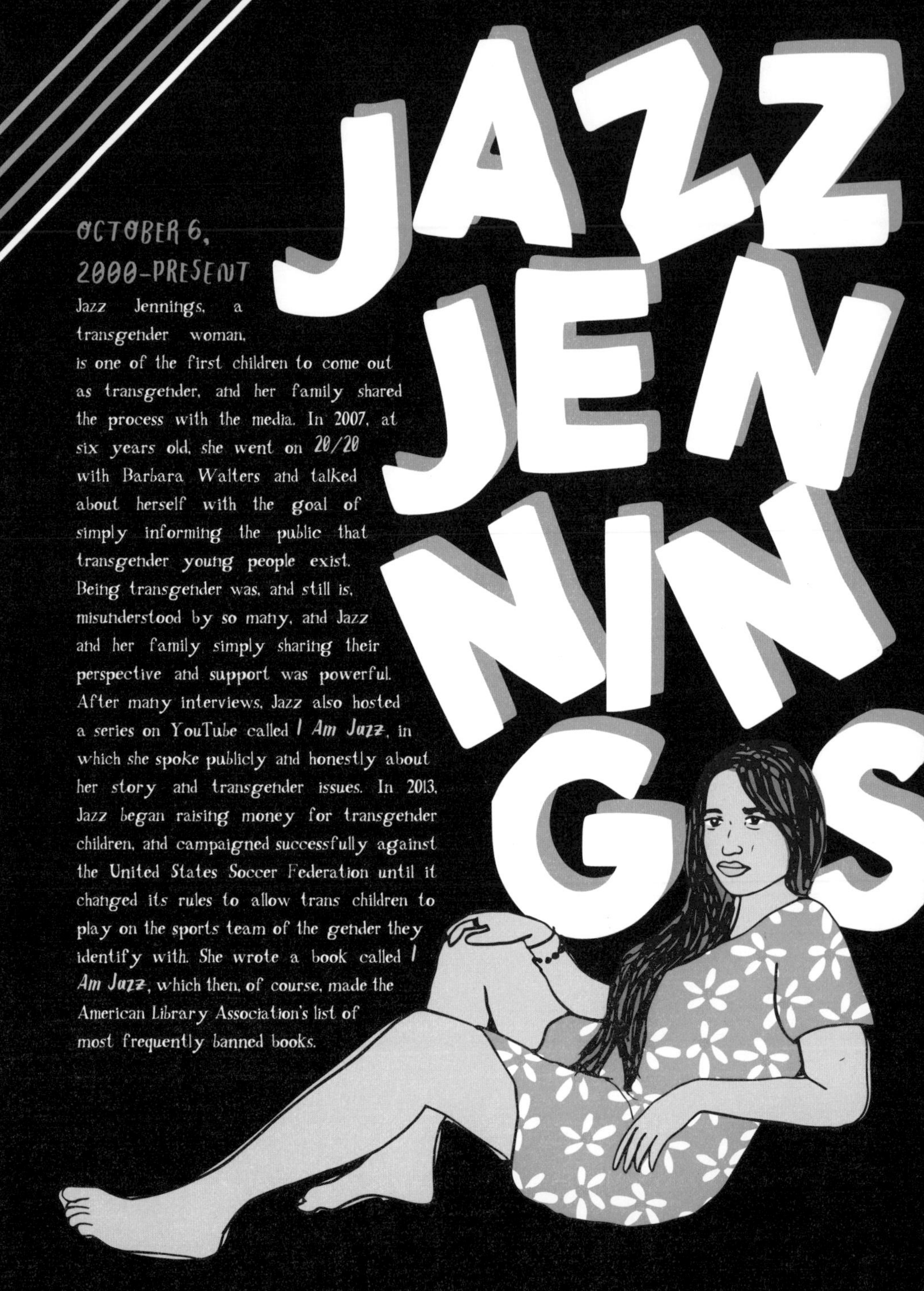

JAZZ JENNINGS

OCTOBER 6, 2000–PRESENT

Jazz Jennings, a transgender woman, is one of the first children to come out as transgender, and her family shared the process with the media. In 2007, at six years old, she went on *20/20* with Barbara Walters and talked about herself with the goal of simply informing the public that transgender young people exist. Being transgender was, and still is, misunderstood by so many, and Jazz and her family simply sharing their perspective and support was powerful. After many interviews, Jazz also hosted a series on YouTube called *I Am Jazz*, in which she spoke publicly and honestly about her story and transgender issues. In 2013, Jazz began raising money for transgender children, and campaigned successfully against the United States Soccer Federation until it changed its rules to allow trans children to play on the sports team of the gender they identify with. She wrote a book called *I Am Jazz*, which then, of course, made the American Library Association's list of most frequently banned books.

2009

RuPaul is a well-known drag queen whose rise to fame was made possible by his outstanding queen-ness, his musical performances, and his participation in campaigns like the MAC AIDS Fund through the 1980s and '90s. He dabbled in acting, music, and filmmaking in the early days, and still does occasionally, but now mainly produces reality shows.

RuPaul's Drag Race is a competitive reality TV show that searches for America's drag superstar each season. Hosted by the marvelous RuPaul himself, the show challenges contestants with tasks in the realm of costumes, modeling, makeup, and the like. Judged by a varying panel each week, the contestants are dismissed from the show one by one in order to find America's next drag superstar. The show premiered in 2009 and is still running, and each season always tops the last. RuPaul won three Emmys in a row for the series in the mid-2010s and has received many other television awards since then. The show has an incredible following, from queens everywhere to queer people alike inspiring individuality and providing perfect and total sass with each episode. *RuPaul's Drag Race* has helped broaden the awareness of drag and the art behind it, also paving the way for very young drag queens like Desmond Is Amazing and Lactatia to follow their dreams sooner, rather than later.

2010s

BARACK OBAMA OBERGEFELL V. HODGES ANN & ROBERT H. LURIE CHILDREN'S HOSPITAL OF CHICAGO LAURA JANE GRACE LAVERNE COX ELLEN PAGE ORANGE IS THE NEW BLACK PULSE NIGHTCLUB QUEER EYE PRIDE TRAIN FRANK OCEAN DANICA ROEM SHARICE DAVIDS POSE JACOB TOBIA THOMAS PAGE MCBEE MURDERS OF BLACK TRANS WOMEN TRANS IN THE MILITARY ALOK VAID-MENON STONEWALL 50 QUEER LIBERATION MARCH

Barack Obama

2010s

Barack Obama, the forty-fourth president of the United States, did the most a president has ever done for the LGBTQ+ community during his eight-year term. His administration was responsible for over 125 changes to policies and regulations in relation to LGBTQ+ protections and rights, as he was the first sitting president to openly support LGBTQ+ rights. Obama was part of the family—he used his power for good when it came to the visibility and safety of queer Americans all over the country and openly supported equality for all. Under Obama, rules like Don't Ask, Don't Tell and the Defense of Marriage Act were repealed, many laws were put into place protecting queer people from discrimination, and many LGBTQ+ people were appointed as ambassadors and officials. In 2016, Obama designated the Stonewall Inn as a national monument, the first to represent the LGBTQ+ community.

2015

On June 26, 2015, the White House lit up *rainbow* as the Supreme Court voted that state bans on same-sex marriages were, in fact, unconstitutional! The case, first heard in August 2014 by a three-judge panel of the U.S. Court of Appeals, addressed two questions: whether same-sex marriage bans *and* the failure of some states to recognize same-sex marriages were constitutional. The court, in a 2–1 decision, decided that it was not unconstitutional to recognize marriage as only between one man and one woman and that it was constitutional for some states to deny legal benefits to same-sex couples who had an out-of-state marriage. The case was immediately brought to the Supreme Court and arguments began on April 28, 2015. Justices Ruth Bader Ginsburg, Sonia Sotomayor, Elena Kagan, Stephen Breyer, and Anthony Kennedy all argued that the right to marry was a fundamental right, and a decision was made—same-sex marriage was now legal! While the institution of marriage may be confusing, it is important to remember that legal marriage entitles couples to a number of benefits: same-sex couples could now adopt in all states, jointly file taxes, be recognized as real "spouses" in case of illness or death, and so on.

Some background on the case itself: Jim Obergefell and John Arthur, an Ohio couple who had been together for twenty-two years, decided to finally marry in 2013, long after the Defense of Marriage Act had passed. At the time, John was extremely sick with ALS and they were unable to travel to a state where they could legally marry. In July 2013, a few months before John died, they flew to Maryland on a medically chartered flight, where they got married inside the plane, as John's declining health would not allow them to leave the plane. When they flew back to Ohio, they found that Jim would not be listed as a spouse on John's death certificate because same-sex marriages were not recognized in Ohio. A district court permitted a temporary restraining order on the ban and allowed Jim's name to be listed on the death certificate when the time came.

Ann + Robert H. Lurie Children's Hospital of Chicago

2013

In 2013, the Ann & Robert H. Lurie Children's Hospital of Chicago launched a new gender-identity-focused program, the first clinic in the Midwest of its kind. During fund-raising, transgender billionaire and investor Jennifer Pritzker matched the donations, helping open what is called the Gender Development Program. The program aids in adolescent gender development, providing services to kids and families who may be questioning their gender identity or know that they are transgender. It provides education on transgender and gender-fluid life, support groups, and help with legal and insurance stuff, all while sustaining high-quality medical care. The program offers services to youth and young adults up to the age of twenty-two, and is not only a hospital, but a community that strives to provide patients and their families with support and care.

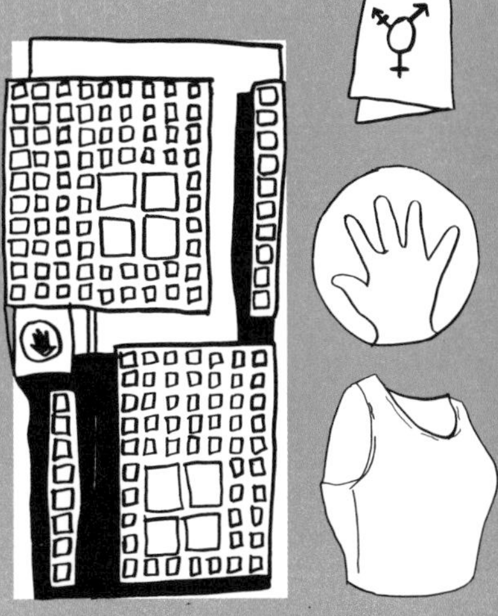

Laura Jane Grace

NOVEMBER 8, 1980–PRESENT

Laura Jane Grace, lead singer of the popular punk band Against Me!, came out as a trans woman in 2012. Coming out brought awareness about trans people to the band's punk fans everywhere. Wishing in secret to really be a woman, Laura Jane Grace struggled with gender dysphoria her whole life. In her early days, she discovered an encyclopedia article about Renée Richards, the trans tennis player, and was inspired and happy to know that people like her existed out there. Laura finally decided to come out as trans after meeting a trans fan who had found truth in the gender-questioning lyrics in one of the band's 2005 songs. After Laura came out and transitioned, Against Me! released an album called ***Transgender Dysphoria Blues***, and Laura also published a tell-all memoir titled ***Tranny: Confessions of Punk Rock's Most Infamous Anarchist Sellout***. Both of these works very publicly shared the journey of Laura's transition. Today, Laura is a huge trans advocate and continues to flourish in her musical career.

Laverne Cox

MAY 29, 1972–PRESENT

Laverne Cox is an actress and trans activist known for her groundbreaking role in *Orange Is the New Black* as Sophia Burset, a trans woman doing time in a women's correctional facility. Laverne has always been in the performance realm, starting her career with dance and then moving to theater when attending Marymount Manhattan College in New York City. Her passions shifted when she discovered her attraction to acting, leading to several trans roles in off-off-Broadway shows and theater productions at her college. Laverne's goals yet again shifted when trans actress Candis Cayne was cast for a recurring role as an actual trans character on *Dirty Sexy Money* in 2007, giving Laverne hope that someday she could also become a successful trans actress. In 2010, Laverne produced her first show on VH1, called *TRANSform Me*, where she and costars Jamie Clayton and Nina Poon gave makeovers to women. When *Orange Is the New Black* came out in 2013, her career really took off, leading to multiple nominations and awards. Her voice in the trans movement is also one of importance, as she is a huge advocate for the transgender community as well as the topic of intersectionality between gender and race.

Ellen Page

FEBRUARY 21, 1987–PRESENT

Ellen Page is a Canadian actress, and an amazing one at that. She's known for her roles in *Juno*, the *X-Men* series, and many other films and shows. Ellen came out as gay in February 2014 at the Human Rights Campaign "Time to Thrive" conference in Las Vegas. In 2016, she and costar Ian Daniel hosted a series on Viceland called *Gaycation*, exploring queer culture in different cities and countries throughout the world! Since coming out, she's been big on activism, whether it be human rights, animal rights, or gay rights, and has been cast in more queer roles in film and TV.

Orange Is the New Black

2013

Orange Is the New Black is a Netflix series based on Piper Kerman's memoir, *Orange Is the New Black: My Year in a Women's Prison*. The show follows character Piper Chapman and her fellow inmates throughout their time in a minimum-security prison after Piper gets busted for drug trafficking and money laundering, focusing on the many lesbian relationships between characters. The show has been running for seven seasons now, and features a range of queer actors including Laverne Cox, Samira Wiley, and Lea DeLaria, among others.

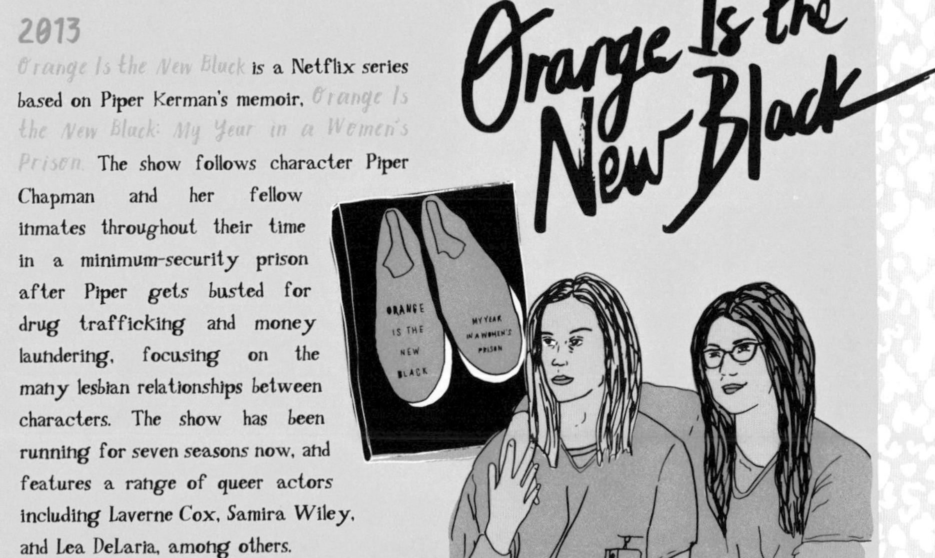

PULSE NIGHT CLUB

Orlando, FL

Pulse was a gay nightclub in Orlando, Florida, owned by Barbara Poma and Ron Legler. Pulse tragically shut its doors in 2016, after the largest mass shooting in the United States at that time. On the night of June 12, 2016, forty-nine members of the LGBTQ+ community were killed and fifty-three were injured by a gunman during a three-hour standoff. The club was opened in 2004 in memory of Barbara's brother, John, who died of AIDS in 1991. It was not only a place to dance and come together as a community while partying under flashing lights and loud music, but a place that spread awareness about prevention of AIDS and breast cancer, immigration rights, and more. The LGBTQ+ and Latinx community lost some of their own that night, but their deaths were not in vain. The following day, Republican Speaker Paul Ryan called for a moment of silence, during which some Democratic representatives who had been pushing for stricter gun laws walked out, shouted at Ryan, and called for legislation. Democratic senators filibustered on the Senate floor for nearly fifteen hours until Congress acted on gun legislation. As a result, the Senate voted on two proposals—one to ban sales of weapons to those on terrorist watch lists, and the other to expand background checks to gun shows and Internet sales. Both measures failed, and the debate over gun control remains a hot topic in American politics.

We also remember them here:

STANLEY ALMODOVAR III, 23 AMANDA ALVEAR, 25 OSCAR A. ARACENA-MONTERO, 26 RODOLFO AYALA-AYALA, 33 ALEJANDRO BARRIOS MARTINEZ, 21 MARTIN BENITEZ TORRES, 33 ANTONIO D. BROWN, 30 DARRYL R. BURT II, 29 JONATHAN A. CAMUY VEGA, 24 ANGEL L. CANDELARIO-PADRO, 28 SIMON A. CARRILLO FERNANDEZ, 31 JUAN CHEVEZ-MARTINEZ, 25 LUIS D. CONDE, 39 CORY J. CONNELL, 21 TEVIN E. CROSBY, 25 FRANKY J. DEJESUS VELAZQUEZ, 50 DEONKA D. DRAYTON, 32 MERCEDEZ M. FLORES, 26 PETER O. GONZALEZ-CRUZ, 22 JUAN R. GUERRERO, 22 PAUL T. HENRY, 41 FRANK HERNANDEZ, 27 MIGUEL A. HONORATO, 30 JAVIER JORGE-REYES, 40 JASON B. JOSAPHAT, 19 EDDIE J. JUSTICE, 30 ANTHONY L. LAUREANO DISLA, 25 CHRISTOPHER A. LEINONEN, 32 BRENDA L. MARQUEZ MCCOOL, 49 JEAN C. MENDEZ PEREZ, 35 AKYRA MONET MURRAY, 18 KIMBERLY MORRIS, 37 JEAN C. NIEVES RODRIGUEZ, 27 LUIS O. OCASIO-CAPO, 20 GERALDO A. ORTIZ-JIMENEZ, 25 ERIC I. ORTIZ-RIVERA, 36 JOEL RAYON PANIAGUA, 32 ENRIQUE L. RIOS JR., 25 JUAN P. RIVERA VELAZQUEZ, 37 YILMARY RODRIGUEZ SOLIVAN, 24 CHRISTOPHER J. SANFELIZ, 24 XAVIER E. SERRANO ROSADO, 35 GILBERTO R. SILVA MENENDEZ, 25 EDWARD SOTOMAYOR JR., 34 SHANE E. TOMLINSON, 33 LEROY VALENTIN FERNANDEZ, 25 LUIS S. VIELMA, 22 LUIS D. WILSON-LEON, 37 JERALD A. WRIGHT, 31

QUEER EYE

2018–PRESENT

In 2018, Netflix brought back *Queer Eye for the Straight Guy* in a revival called *Queer Eye*, and we all literally cannot. The Fab Five were recast as a younger, more diverse crew following the same premise as the original—in each episode, the Fab Five take on a life-makeover project. But this newer series focuses much more on self-love and living to your fullest potential. The episodes in the new seasons, described as "more than a makeover," include a varied selection of women, men, transgender people, and more. Every episode 100 percent inspires tears and good feelings, revealing hardships and struggles from the person being made over as well as the personal stories of the cast. The new Fab Five cast includes Antoni Porowski, Food; Jonathan Van Ness, Grooming; Bobby Berk, Design; Tan France, Fashion; and Karamo Brown, Culture. This reboot of *Queer Eye* couldn't have come at a better time—aside from it being a fun reality makeover show, it's become an important milestone in actual queer representation in the media, in a real and raw way.

Pride Train

Service Information

All Times

365 days
24 hours a day

No bigotry, hatred, or prejudice allowed at this station at any time.

Travel alternative:

This train only moves forward.

Reminder:

Your homophobia is probably just a phase.

2017

Pride Train service announcement posters began popping up in NYC subway stations in 2017, designed by Thomas Shim, Jack Welles, and Ezequiel Consoli as a response to bigotry and hate crimes, and what better way than to pull a Keith Haring and advertise in one of the most public of spaces: the subway. The posters are designed to look like actual MTA service posters, although here's the kicker: Pride Train is not part of the MTA! These guerrilla-style service posters promote LGBTQ+ acceptance and love, with witty sayings like "No bigotry, hatred, or prejudice allowed at this station at any time." Hilarious travel alternative suggestions include "Get over it," "Take a Jamaica Center–bound LIRR train. Transfer to a JFK Airport AirTrain. Buy a one-way plane ticket that takes you far, far away," and "¯_(ツ)_/¯". This is one group of amazing people starting a conversation about queer and minority acceptance, batting away homophobia and violence against people of color, and creating little reminders all throughout the city that we queers are everywhere.

FRANK OCEAN

OCTOBER 28, 1987–PRESENT

Frank Ocean is an R&B and hip-hop artist, writer, and producer. He started his career ghostwriting, eventually joined Odd Future in 2010, and finally broke out into his own solo career as well. In 2012, after some speculation about his sexuality, Ocean posted a letter titled "Frank Ocean: My First Love Was a Man" on Tumblr. He talks about his feelings for a friend and the intimacy that they shared. While Frank Ocean is not the first in the R&B world to come out as anything other than straight, it is a genre that has been dominated by straight men and is often riddled with casual homophobia. Additionally, his story does not use labels—he talks about loving a man, but doesn't identify himself as gay or bisexual. He simply talks about himself, love, and the complex feelings that come with it.

SEPTEMBER 30, 1984–PRESENT

Danica Roem is a Democratic politician who, in 2018, became the first-ever transgender person to serve on the Virginia General Assembly, and the first to run openly as a trans woman for any U.S. state legislature. Her background is in journalism, but she decided to run for political office after Republican Bob Marshall opposed same-sex marriage and proposed a "bathroom bill" to force transgender people to use bathrooms corresponding to their assigned sex at birth. Oh yeah, and he'd been in office for twelve terms and proudly called himself the state's "chief homophobe." As expected, Danica's campaign faced a ton of transphobic discrimination from her opponent and the general public. She ended up winning the election with 53.72 percent of the votes. Take that!

MAY 22, 1980–PRESENT

Sharice Davids is also a Democratic politician, who has served as a U.S. representative for Kansas since 2019. She's racked up the firsts: first openly LGBTQ+ Native American elected to Congress and first openly LGBTQ+ person to serve in Congress from Kansas, a notoriously conservative state. She's the *second* Native American to represent Kansas in Congress, but first Native American woman! Sharice Davids is not only a politician, but an attorney and former professional mixed martial arts fighter.

2018

Pose is a TV series that delves deep into the ball culture of the 1980s and '90s in New York City, featuring the largest transgender cast in television history. Touching on themes including AIDS, drag, balls, houses, and chosen families, *Pose* will teach you about a culture that has long been around but has yet to be discovered by many Americans. Created by Ryan Murphy, Brad Falchuk, and Steven Canals, the show is glittery, eye-catching, and deep with emotion and struggle between the characters, making it an educational and emotional representation of part of the queer community that remains important to this day.

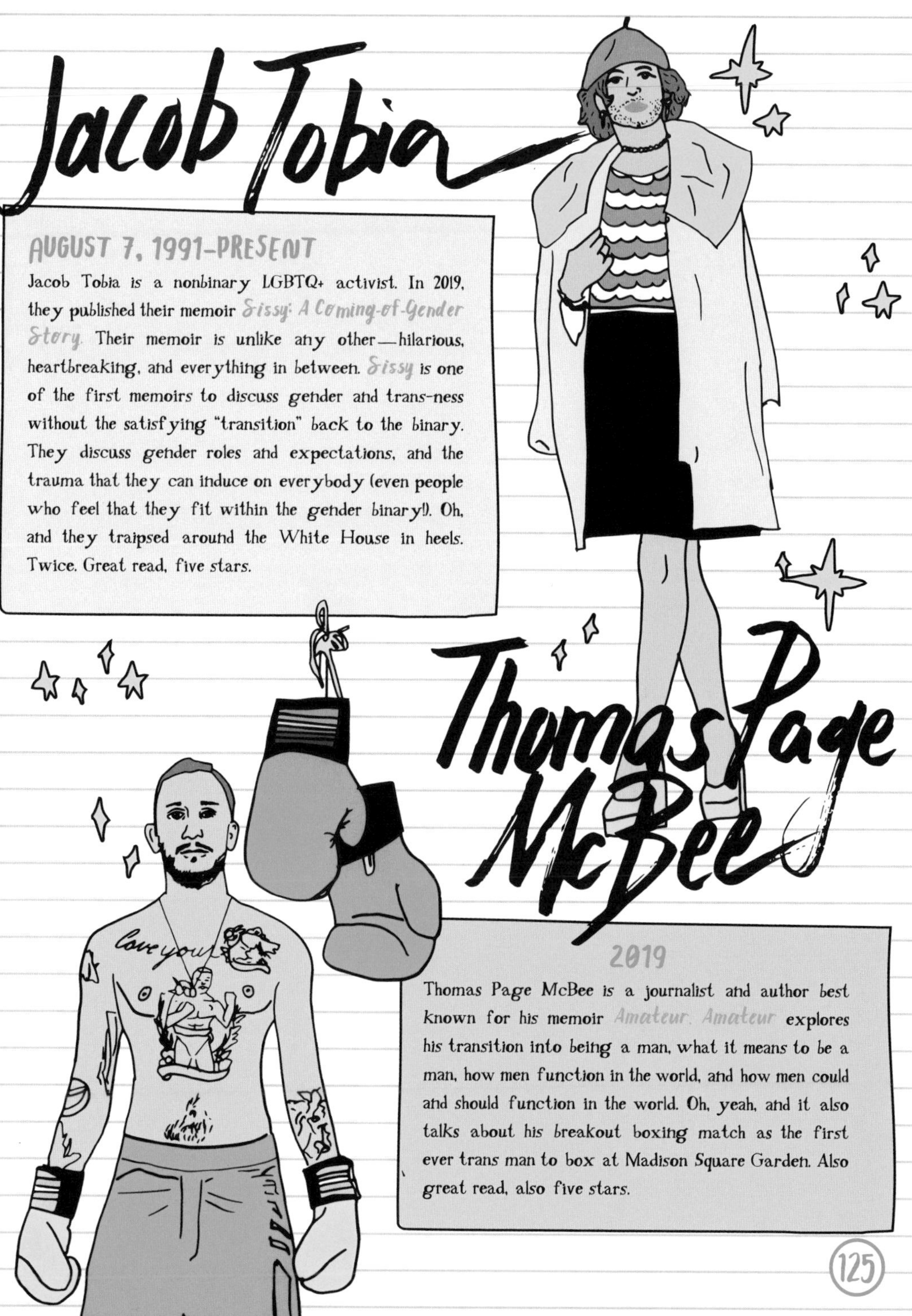

Jacob Tobia

AUGUST 7, 1991–PRESENT

Jacob Tobia is a nonbinary LGBTQ+ activist. In 2019, they published their memoir *Sissy: A Coming-of-Gender Story*. Their memoir is unlike any other—hilarious, heartbreaking, and everything in between. *Sissy* is one of the first memoirs to discuss gender and trans-ness without the satisfying "transition" back to the binary. They discuss gender roles and expectations, and the trauma that they can induce on everybody (even people who feel that they fit within the gender binary!). Oh, and they traipsed around the White House in heels. Twice. Great read, five stars.

Thomas Page McBee

2019

Thomas Page McBee is a journalist and author best known for his memoir *Amateur*. *Amateur* explores his transition into being a man, what it means to be a man, how men function in the world, and how men could and should function in the world. Oh, yeah, and it also talks about his breakout boxing match as the first ever trans man to box at Madison Square Garden. Also great read, also five stars.

MURDERS OF BLACK TRANS WOMEN

2010s

At the time of writing this (June 2019), there have already been eleven murders of black trans women so far *this year*. This is an epidemic, a systematic pattern of deadly violence against trans women of color. The most recent, the killing of Muhlaysia Booker, demonstrates an utter disregard and ultimate hatred for both black bodies and transgender bodies. Booker was involved in a traffic incident in April, after which she was beaten in broad daylight by a man named Edward Thomas as he yelled homophobic slurs. Thomas was charged with aggravated assault, but not a hate crime, as gender identity is not covered in many states' hate crime statutes, including Texas's. In the attack, Booker suffered a concussion and a fractured wrist. One month later, she was fatally shot.

Booker's story is familiar—transgender women of color face disproportionately high rates of violence. Despite trans visibility rising, with celebrities coming out and more people identifying off the gender binary, violence against the community is rising even faster. The count of trans women of color murdered is not even exact, due to failures of underreporting or the misgendering of victims by family members or the media. While it is hard to pinpoint an exact cause of this high rate of violence, it is likely a deadly mixture of misogyny, transphobia, and racism, all combined into one ugly rage.

Additionally, trans people can face higher rates of violence because they are often turned away by family, homeless shelters, and churches; they also face unequal opportunity for justice, jobs, education, health care, and so on, and often have to resort to prostitution or other crime. Police, who should be keeping people safe, are often the source of additional systemic violence against trans people. Someone who is locked up for a petty crime may be housed in a jail that corresponds to their assigned sex at birth, not to their gender identity; which puts trans people in extreme danger. For example, Layleen Polanco Xtravaganza died alone in solitary confinement at Rikers Island. She had been arrested on misdemeanor charges, but could not afford the five-hundred-dollar bail, so she was sent to jail. Two months later, she was dead, and as of the time this book is being written, no cause of death has been determined. This is one example of the risks and vulnerabilities of transgender people once they face incarceration—solitary confinement, failure to receive adequate medical care, and so on. Outside of jail, many trans people may be denied health care due to anti-trans bias, or because they are profiled as sex workers. Violence against trans women of

color lies at an unfortunate intersection of anti-LGBTQ+ violence, systemic racism, misogyny, anti-immigration bias, and other structural systems of oppression.

How can you help? Speak up for trans people of color. Hire them for jobs. Pay them. Make space for their voices. Hold people accountable for casual transphobia.

As of June 2019, we remember these women killed this year—keeping in mind that there may be many more by the time this book comes out, and that this list does not include people whose deaths weren't reported, murders that were reported as suicides, or victims who were unnamed by the media.

DANA MARTIN

JAZZALINE WARE

ASHANTI CARMON

MUHLAYSIA BOOKER

CLAIRE LEGATO

MICHELLE "TAMIKA" WASHINGTON

PARIS CAMERON

CHYNAL LINDSEY

CHANEL SCURLOCK

ZOE SPEARS

BROOKLYN LINDSEY

Trans in the Military 2019

In 2017, Trump made a typically inflammatory tweet stating that transgender people would no longer be allowed to serve in the military. The tweet sparked national protests, and implied that trans people were a burden on the military's resources. On April 12, 2019, an actual policy took effect that denied transgender personnel the right to serve unless they enlist under their sex assigned at birth.

Some background: For most of American history, there was no ban. But there was also no real talk of transgender people, and often women who wanted to serve dressed as men in order to "pass" as men. In 1960, the executive order that banned gays and lesbians from serving in the government was expanded to include gender identity and the military, and was in effect until June 30, 2016. For most of Obama's presidency, anybody with a history of psychosexual disturbance was not allowed to serve—this put transgender people in the same category as exhibitionists, voyeurs, and people with other paraphilias. However, Obama repealed the transgender ban in 2016; his secretary of defense, Ashton Carter, and the American Medical Association were in favor of the repeal. From June 30, 2016, until April 11, 2019, trans people were allowed to serve eighteen months after completing a medical transition.

Between 2016 and Trump's tweet, Vicky Hartzler, a Republican from Missouri, researched the health care costs of transgender service personnel and concluded that transgender people seeking gender reassignment surgery would be too costly for the military budget—because the military notoriously does not overspend (lol). Hartzler failed to understand that not every trans person seeks gender-affirming surgery, and she also grossly overestimated the number of transgender personnel serving. However, when faced with the facts, she said she felt "very confident" in her faulty research. Due to the high costs, she proposed an amendment to the National Defense Authorization Act that would discharge all transgender military personnel. The amendment was rejected. Twice!

As usual, much to the surprise of White House officials, Trump hastily made an announcement via tweet that trans people were indeed not allowed to serve due to the burden of medical costs. However, the ban was clearly motivated by transphobia and full of incorrect, debunked research. The ban insinuates that trans people are mentally ill and that caring for their mental health is expensive and would create difficulties during combat.

Trans people are not mentally ill. The ban implies that trans people are a huge burden to the budget—when a 2016 study by the RAND Corporation shows that trans medical costs such as gender-affirming surgery comprise between 0.005 and 0.017 percent of the Defense Department's health care budget. Keep in mind that the Defense Department's health care covers Viagra—according to the *Washington Post*, the department spends over $41.6 million on Viagra per year, whereas gender-affirming surgery for *every* transgender person would cost only $8.4 million at the very most (and they don't all request it). The ban implies that trans troops would disrupt military readiness—service members who had recently had surgery would not be able to deploy, or service members undergoing gender-affirming surgery might upset their unit-mates. The ban was made on faulty assumptions and vehemently opposed by top military experts, and is only another incident of transphobia and anti-trans hysteria that marks how much further our community has to go, despite all the progress that we have already made.

Military Spending

"We need a budget cut!"

$41.6 million on Viagra
$8.4 million gender affirming surgery

Alok Vaid-Menon

JULY 1, 1991–PRESENT

Alok Vaid-Menon is a gender-nonconforming performance artist, spoken word poet, and LGBTQ+ activist. They are from an Indian American family, and their powerful poetry often explores the intersections of being trans/gender-nonconforming and a person of color, and the shame, trauma, and systemic violence that come with that identity. They have also released a fashion collection in India, which prominently features colorful printed skirts and dresses. If you tune into their Instagram, you can catch them in fun, bright colors with a standout lip color!

STONEWALL 50

The year 2019 marked the fiftieth anniversary of the Stonewall riots, the night that is said to be the turning point in the gay liberation movement. Combining the commemoration of the riots with WorldPride, NYC went hard with pride month, hosting millions of visitors from all over the world. On June 28, 2019, the actual anniversary of the riots, there was a Stonewall commemorative rally outside the Stonewall Inn, featuring speakers and advocates for the LGBTQ+ community. The Heritage of Pride parade took place the following Sunday, and was real rainbow and real queer. Since the first parade in 1970, the NYC pride march, among many others around the country, has grown in attendance and support, such as sponsorship by businesses. Pride month is a magical thing, and it is even more magical when you realize how many of us there actually are. We really are everywhere, and if not for the queens and queers at the Stonewall Inn that late night in the sixties, we wouldn't be fifty years into seeing the changes and acceptance that the LGBTQ+ community has achieved along the way.

QUEER LIB

On the same day as the WorldPride parade, the Queer Liberation March traced the steps of the original Christopher Street Liberation Day March of 1970, processing from Sheridan Square to Bryant Park, and then to the Great Lawn in Central Park, picking up supporters along he way. This march, led by the Reclaim Pride Coalition, was meant to be a counter to the corporate/capitalist themes of WorldPride. There were no corporations handing out rainbow keychains, no police dancing in the street, no rainbow floats, just a rally in the park to celebrate those that we have lost along he way—trans women of color, people who lied in the AIDS crisis, missing and murdered ndigenous women, and international LGBTQ+ people who live in danger and without rights n their countries—and to rally around the work that our community still has left. The Queer Liberation March was not afraid to call out the capitalist interests of corporations, and the fact that many companies hand out rainbow items during June but do nothing else to help the LGBTQ+ community. At the rally, notable speakers from the community made their messages clear. Larry Kramer, ason L. Walker, Black Trans Media Founders Sasha Alexander and Olympia Perez, Staceyann Chin, Cecilia Gentili, and many more were among the speakers at he event, and all reiterated the message that the work in the LGBTQ+ community is no done while we have people in camps, whil we have black trans women being murdere at such a high rate, while we deny healt care to many, while we criminalize sex workers, and so on. This march focused o combating transphobia, racism, classism, an other forms of oppression that keep other down throughout the world, and advocate for an end to ICE and the prison-industria complex that keeps people down and enable systems of racism and bigotry. It seeks to go back to the roots of the march—no a parade to show off rainbows. In 1969, th patrons of the Stonewall Inn fought back and rioted against systemic violence, in th same period as other countercultural rebellions The Stonewall protest was focused on th LGBTQ+ community, but was inherently intersectional as it coincided with th anti-war and black liberation movement. *All* oppression is connected, and the Quee Liberation March made that clear. It is no a one-time movement; anybody intereste in joining the Reclaim Pride Coalition may attend a next-steps meeting, information o which can be found on the coalition's website

ATiON MARCH

YEARBOOK

LADY GAGA
SINGER

SAPPHIRE
POET AND AUTHOR

CARA DELEVINGNE
MODEL AND ACTRESS

RICKY MARTIN
SINGER

CARRIE BROWNSTEIN
SINGER/SONGWRITER/ACTRESS/
COMEDIAN

AMANDLA STENBERG
ACTRESS

ROSIE O'DONNELL
COMEDIAN

LANCE BASS
SINGER

ST. VINCENT
AKA ANNIE CLARK
MUSICIAN AND PRODUCER

MARGARET CHO
COMEDIAN

JANELLE MONÁE
SINGER/SONGWRITER/
ACTRESS/PRODUCER

MILEY CYRUS
SINGER/SONGWRITER/ACTRESS

KING PRINCESS
AKA MIKAELA STRAUS
SINGER

CHRIS COLFER
ACTOR

TIM COOK
CEO OF APPLE

CYNTHIA NIXON
ACTRESS

JODIE FOSTER
ACTRESS

ANDERSON COOPER
JOURNALIST AND TV PERSONALITY

ELTON JOHN
MUSICIAN

HAYLEY KIYOKO
SINGER/SONGWRITER/ACTRESS

ABBI JACOBSON
ACTRESS/COMEDIAN

CHAZ BONO
PERFORMER

SARAH PAULSON
ACTRESS/DIRECTOR/PRODUCER

IAN ALEXANDER
ACTOR

NEIL PATRICK HARRIS
ACTOR

WANDA SYKES
COMEDIAN

GEORGE TAKEI
ACTOR

This next section serves as a sort of handbook or informational section. It contains definitions of words that may describe you or someone you know. It contains information on what it's like to transition if you choose to. Or how to have safe sex. Think of this section as a handbook, with the purpose of navigating your queerness or understanding someone else's.

GAY
IS
GOOD
NYC

Simplified for your ultimate enjoyment and comprehension, here are some important terms to help you navigate the queer community the right way! Quite a few of the words we use today have been repurposed by the LGBTQ+ community, as some were once (and sometimes still are) used in a rude and offensive way. Although not everyone embraces "queer" and "dyke" in an affirming way, you should always be respectful of the words someone chooses and DOESN'T choose to use to identify themselves. A huge reason for LGBTQ+ people turning radical and demanding equal treatment was, and still is, reclaiming once hurtful words and making them their own. We have the power.

Ally *noun* A friend of the LGBTQ+ community! This term typically refers to any straight or non-queer person who supports the LGBTQ+ community, and is often used with friends, activists, and advocates of oppressed groups.

Androgynous *adjective* Blurring the line between "masculine" and "feminine." Androgynous style was possibly a contributor to the start of the fall of gender binaries. Think Bowie and Tilda Swinton.

Asexual *adjective* In simple terms, not feeling the need to have sex, or not feeling sexual desire.

Bi-curious *adjective* Curious about exploring sexual relationships with people who are not the usual gender they are attracted to.

Binding *verb* Flattening the chest with cloth or tight clothes to present a male-like appearance. Chest binding is a way for trans men to curb dysphoria.

Bisexual, Bi *adjective* Attracted emotionally and sexually to both male and female genders.

Butch *noun, adjective* A "masculine" lesbian, or an adjective to describe a lesbian who has traditional traits of a male.

Camp, Campy *noun, adjective* An aesthetic introduced to the queer community as early as the 1900s. Often associated with drag, this vibe could be described as effeminate, exaggerated, theatrical. Think John Waters, RuPaul. Further reading: "Notes on 'Camp,'" by Susan Sontag.

Cisgender *adjective* Having a gender identity that matches one's assigned sex at birth.

Closet, Closeted *noun, adjective* A place where secretly queer people hang out, sometimes by choice, sometimes for fear of rejection. Some closeted people don't even realize they're in the closet, either. Often associated with coming out, as in the phrase "coming out of the closet."

Coming out *verb* When a queer person announces their queerness to the world! Or just to themselves or to anyone they care about. Coming out is essentially acknowledging your queerness. Hey, wait, when do straight people come out?

Drag *noun* Clothing or style that is generally of the opposite gender and a bit more campy. A more updated term for "cross-dressing," which is outdated and also considered quite offensive these days. Dressing in drag is popular for

entertainment and self-expression.

Drag king *noun* Usually a female-identifying person dressing in men's clothes.

Drag queen *noun* Usually a male-identifying person dressing in women's clothes. Often glittery, exaggerated, and fabulous AF. Work.

Dyke *noun* Slang nickname for "lesbian" that was once used insultingly, but has been adopted by radical lesbians who have tried to turn the term around as a more positive word.

Femme *noun* A lesbian whose appearance is more "feminine" by gender binary standards.

Fluid, Fluidity *adjective* Ever-changing, shifting, not fixed or stable. This can be in reference to one's sexuality, i.e., sexually fluid, meaning their sexual orientation isn't just one way or can be subject to change over time. Genderfluidity is when one is fluid with their gender, whether it be floating to, from, or between male, female, and neither to feel out what is comfortable for them. *See also the Gender Identity section on page 160.*

Gay *noun, adjective* Someone who is attracted to those of the same gender as their own. This word is not really applicable to the entire LGBTQ+ community but is often used as an umbrella term despite its lack of inclusion of other groups in the spectrum. While its origin is hard to pinpoint, many speculate that the word "gay," also meaning "happy," was used as a code word for gays to be aware of each other back when it was basically illegal to be gay. It eventually replaced "homosexual," which is now an outdated and somewhat offensive way to describe someone who identifies as gay.

Gender binary *noun* The concept that there are only two genders, male and female, and that if you are born one or the other biologically, you will or should be a masculine male or a feminine female. This concept is closed-minded and so twenty years ago.

Gender dysphoria *noun* The pain and confusion that one experiences when their assigned sex at birth does not match their gender identity. For example, someone assigned female at birth who identifies as trans or gender nonconforming may feel dysphoric when a pair of jeans clings tightly to their wide hips.

Gender expression *noun* The external expression of the gender you choose to identify with, based on socially defined behaviors and fashion.

Genderqueer *adjective, noun* Identifying as neither male nor female. This can be used interchangeably with ***gender nonconforming***, ***gender neutral***, and ***gender nonbinary***. Being any of these things doesn't mean that you are trans. Being genderqueer just means that you don't stick to one gender's societal roles and constructs consistently. An example of this might be a woman working as a mechanic, or a man being interested in sewing. In a way, we're all genderqueer based on our diverse interests and hobbies that were once and still sometimes are associated with typical gender binaries!

Heterosexual *adjective, noun* Attracted sexually and emotionally to the opposite sex, primarily associated with male-female relationships. In less scientific terms, this is what a ***straight*** person is.

Homophobia *noun* Fear of gays and lesbians, fueled by talk that they're sexual deviants and unnatural. "Prejudice" is also an accurate word to describe homophobia.

Homosexual *adjective, noun* Attracted to the same sex as one's own. This outdated term is still used today, mostly to describe the history of the LGBTQ+ community, but previously was employed in a very disparaging way toward the gay community. In the present day, churches often use this word when denouncing the LGBTQ+ community. This word is not recommended and should be removed from your vocabulary completely.

Intersex *noun, adjective* Someone born with any variations in sex characteristics—which can include chromosomes, hormones, or genitals—that do not fit the typical binary notion of male and female.

Lesbian *noun, adjective* Anyone who identifies as a woman who is attracted to others who identify as women.

Nonbinary *adjective* Having a gender identity or sexual orientation that does not fit into the gender constructs of male or female norms. *See also* Genderqueer.

Out *adjective* Being open about one's sexual orientation and/or gender identity to oneself and the public, possibly even in one's professional life. Or, as we like to say, living your best life!

Outing *verb* Intentionally revealing someone's queerness without their consent. Outing is a very inconsiderate thing to do, so if you're considering outing anyone anytime soon, DON'T. It's not your place!

Pansexual *noun, adjective* Someone who is attracted to people regardless of their sex or gender identity.

Partner *noun* A gender-neutral way to describe your significant other, rather than using gender binary terms such as girlfriend, boyfriend, wife, husband, etc....

Queen *noun* Not to be confused with "drag queen," "queen" was once an offensive term to describe more flamboyant and effeminate gay men, but is now used more as a term of endearment between gays.

Queer *adjective* Once a slur for gay and lesbian, "queer" is now being turned around as an all-encompassing umbrella term for the LGBTQ+ community. Although not everyone in the community agrees with adopting this once hurtful word to be a positive descriptor, many younger people have welcomed the identity of queer with open arms. Identifying as queer also puts less pressure on committing to a more specific label, such as lesbian, bi, trans, etc....

Questioning *verb* Exploring one's sexuality and/or gender identity. This doesn't just go for straight people experimenting with the same gender—it can apply to all genders and all sexual orientations.

Sexual orientation *noun* The scientifically accurate way to describe someone's sexual and emotional attraction to another gender. An outdated version of this is "sexual preference," which is quite offensive as it insinuates that being queer is a choice. One might further argue that acting on it is a choice, but we didn't choose to feel this way.

Straight *adjective* A more casual term for "heterosexual." *See* Heterosexual.

Transgender, Trans *adjective* Having a gender identity that does not match completely one's assigned sex at birth.

Transphobia *noun* Fear of transgender people, which 100 percent translates as hatred toward an oppressed people.

Two-Spirit *noun, adjective* An umbrella term used by Native people to describe someone whose body simultaneously houses both a masculine and a feminine spirit. They fall outside the male and female binary, and occupy a third gender.

Lesbians come in all different shapes, sizes, colors, and styles. Gender identity, the way you present yourself when it comes to lesbianism, is super diverse. The spectrum ranges from super femme to butch to androgynous to nonbinary—there is no correct way to be a lesbian; there are, like, a million ways to be a lesbian.

Fun history lesson on a well-known lesbian stereotype: you must have U-Haul on your speed dial, next to your girlfriend AND your ex. The concept of U-Hauling has been around for quite some time. Not familiar with the U-Haul joke? Comic Lea DeLaria is often credited as the source of the joke: "What does a lesbian bring to a second date? A U-Haul." As early as the 1950s, women in lesbian relationships found it easy to hide their relationships from the public eye in the safety of their own homes. Being gay back then wasn't as easy as it is today; sometimes moving in together was a safer bet so that at least they could be themselves at home. Even Leslie Feinberg, author of classic recommended reading **Stone Butch Blues**, can vouch for this U-Hauling trait of lesbian couples. Lesbian relationships can go from 0 to 100 really quickly, meaning that you and your new boo are each other's priorities 100 percent, 24/7.

Although nowadays the term "gay" is more often associated specifically with men attracted to men, "gay" back in the day was more of an umbrella term for the LGBTQ+ community, sort of like how today's term "queer" is a more simple and all-encompassing word for all groups within the spectrum. Before queers were called gays, they were called homosexuals. As you've read in the earlier sections, the term "homosexual" was associated with sexual deviance, in part because of the American Psychiatric Association's deeming homosexuality a mental illness in 1952. The APA later removed it from its list of mental illnesses, about a decade or so into the transition into the word "gay." But "homosexual" still had a negative stigma to it, and the "homosexuals" didn't want to put up with it, as they shouldn't have to. Another concern about the term "homosexual" was that it characterized gay people only as "sexual" people. During the start of the homophile movement, the gays wanted to separate the "sexual" part from themselves.

"Gay" was used as a code word at first, so that other gays could talk about gay stuff in front of straight people without letting on about their sexual orientation. "Gay" ultimately took quite a while to become a mainstream term, and "homosexual" is still used to describe the LGBTQ+ community on many media platforms and in general conversation among people who are usually homophobes, or just don't know any better.

"Gay" is still somewhat used as an umbrella term today, though "queer" is more inclusive, as "gay" has shifted more toward referring to men. Gay men are practically a category of their own, though a vast and diverse one. There are flamboyant gays, leather gays, bear gays, the list goes on.

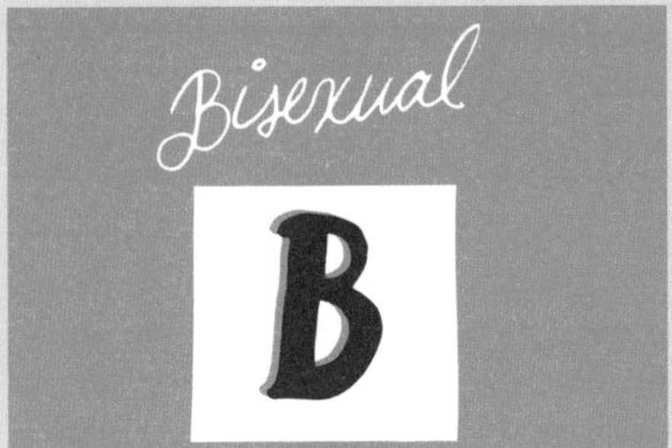

Bisexuality is when someone is attracted to both genders, because we're all a little gay! The concept of bisexuality is often shot down by the queer community, with statements like "pick a side already" or "you can't have both." NOT TRUE. Although bisexual people can essentially flow back and forth between partaking in well-accepted heteronormative relationships and suffering from the annoying homophobic struggles of being in a queer relationship, people who identify as bisexual hold a special quality that not all of us do—the ability to love both guys and gals simultaneously. It's not selfish, it's not weird, it's truly a gift to be able to see past the physical constraints of gender. The same goes for pansexual-identifying people, but you can find more about that in the "pansexual" section. The concept of bisexuality has been around since ancient Greek times, just as gay relationships have been. Bisexuality was formerly grouped with homosexuality as a mental illness. The Kinsey scale, promoted in the 1950s by Alfred Kinsey, really helped the idea of bisexuality come into the mainstream.

Transgender

T

"Transgender" has many different meanings. You see, the prefix "trans" means "beyond," "across," or "through." Think of a transatlantic flight: it goes across the Atlantic Ocean. Gender is so complicated, and socially stigmatized, that "transgender" can be used to describe anyone who does not identify fully with their assigned gender at birth. The opposite of "transgender" is "cisgender"—anyone who ***does*** identify with their assigned gender at birth. Many people hear "transgender" and think it involves a hard transition—that you have to go from male to female, or vice versa. But it's so much more than that. It can include people who are nonbinary, genderqueer, or agender. Some trans people ***do*** choose to transition from one binary to the other, with or without surgery. Some trans people simply exist in the in-between of gender. After all, gender is a social construct.

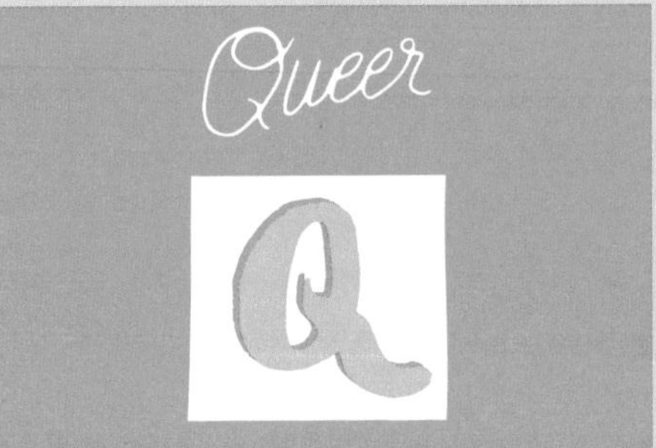

"Queer" is practically an umbrella term for the LGBTQ+ spectrum—in other words, a really easy way to say you're anything other than cis-hetero. Many people take on this identity, rather than narrowing it down to a more specific title like lesbian, or pansexual, or even transgender. Literally anyone who identifies with the LGBTQ+ community can use this category because of its vagueness and openness to interpretation. The word "queer" wasn't always liked throughout the community, and even today people debate whether or not it should be used as a descriptor due to its history as a slur. But many millennials, Gen Xers, and baby boomers alike have adopted the term as their own, a prime example of taking something that was once harmful and negative to the community and reclaiming it as something positive.

The questioning period in a person's life doesn't necessarily mean that they are "going through a phase," or "just confused," as closed-minded people like to put it, but rather it represents a moment when you are not quite sure what you want or who you are when it comes to your sexuality or gender identity. Questioning is completely, 100 percent normal. Almost everyone in the LGBTQ+ community faces this time in their lives. Questioning doesn't have to mean physically experimenting, either; it can simply mean consideration and acknowledgment of life and romance different from what you are used to. It is common that the questioning period happens during college years, a fresh start in a new life on your own, with new rules, or lack thereof, or after a move to somewhere new. Some questioning folks may not have even considered that they could be queer until much later in their lives. If you aren't really exposed to the culture of the queer community, it may not even occur to you until way down the line that maybe you aren't straight, or even cis for that matter. Questioning is a time for exploration, finding yourself, and learning about other people in the process. It is life changing for some, having that great realization that there is more to life than you thought, more than what you were taught growing up or just assumed because of your surroundings. It's totally a magical time.

Someone who is born intersex has sexual anatomy that does not typically match either female or male—this could mean that they were born with genital ambiguity or chromosomal differences. Intersexuality used to be known as hermaphroditism. One huge issue that intersex people face is that most states, aside from a few that now offer a third gender option, require a family or doctor to indicate "male" or "female" on a birth certificate. However, someone with ambiguous sexual anatomy may not fit into either of these boxes. Many families choose to hormonally or surgically "correct" the anomaly to align their baby's gender with a socially acceptable "male" or "female" identity, which may be premature. Someone who was born intersex may have had the wrong sex "chosen" for them at birth. Ideally, no medical intervention should be made on an intersex person, especially at birth, so that they can make the choice for themselves as they grow older.

If "pansexual" sounds a lot like "bisexual," that's because it's similar! One key difference, though, is that "pansexual" emphasizes ***any*** gender identity, while the term "bisexual" is still tied to the gender binary (that is, I like either boys ***or*** girls, without acknowledging any other identity). This is important, though! The term pansexual encompasses any gender identity, of which there are many.

"Two-Spirit" is a term used by Native Americans to describe someone who fits in both masculine and feminine gender roles. Before European colonization, Native Americans celebrated Two-Spirit people and a wide variety of genders and sexualities. While Two-Spirit Natives always existed, the term was coined in 1990 at a Native American/First Nations LGBTQ+ conference as a way to distinctly separate LGBTQ+ Native Americans from non-Native LGBTQ+ folks.

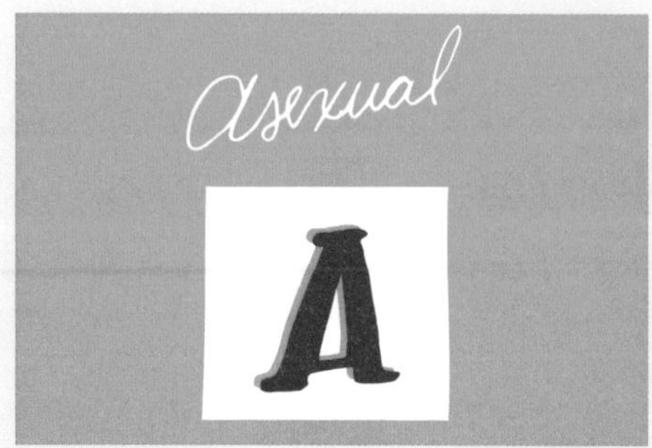

Despite the lack of desire for sexual activity, people who are asexual may still experience romantic feelings toward any gender identity. They are not necessarily aromantic. While it sounds black and white, an asexual person may still get married to any gender, may have sex with any gender, may fall in love with any gender, and so on. Or they may not! In many cases, an asexual person can fall in love without or with varying sexual attraction.

Typically, androgyny has to do with gender presentation, or the outward expression of expected gender roles. This is complicated, because "presenting" as female or male has so much to do with gender norms, which are so problematic.

PRIDE FLAGS

The most prominent pride flag today is the simplified variation of Gilbert Baker's rainbow flag, with stripes of red, orange, yellow, green, blue, and purple. The flag was designed in response to the growing awareness of LGBTQ+ folks in the 1970s, as queers everywhere were in need of a symbolic representation of their community. However, the rainbow flag is not the only pride flag in the mix: there are several other flags out there, all designed for more specific groups of people that fall under the LGBTQ+ category. Think of it like this: You know how there is the American flag that represents the country as a whole, and then each state has its own flag, like California's trendy bear flag, and so on. Well, imagine that the rainbow pride flag is the American flag of the queer community, and all of its subcategories, like transgender, asexual, leather, nonbinary, lesbian, etc., are all the states with their own sub-flags. It is not a competition and in no way a means to divide the community, but it is a way to accommodate more specific communities under the LGBTQ+ umbrella. Each flag has its own array of colors, symbols, and meanings, making them really unique. Flag propositions by all types of members of the LGBTQ+ community are contributed frequently, so we wouldn't be surprised if there were several new flags added to the mix in the next year!

RAINBOW PRIDE FLAG, by Gilbert Baker, **1978:** Pink for sexuality, red for life, orange for healing, yellow for the sun, green for nature, turquoise for art, blue for harmony, violet for the soul.

TRADITIONAL GAY PRIDE FLAG, 1979: Pink and turquoise were eventually dropped from the flag due to fabric shortages of the colors.

PHILADELPHIA PRIDE FLAG, 2017: Created for the campaign More Color More Pride to recognize non-white LGBTQ+ members by adding a black and brown stripe above the traditional rainbow stripes. Many people were against this edit to the flag, as they argued that the original rainbow flag never had anything to do with race. Sounds like someone's jealous there's no designated white history month.

PROGRESS PRIDE FLAG, by Daniel Quasar, **2018:** A response to the Philadelphia Pride Flag, with the trans flag included in it, aiming to highlight the progress made with all groups within the LGBTQ+ community.

GENDERFLUID FLAG, by JJ Poole, **2012:** An all-gender-encompassing flag. Pink for femininity; purple for androgyny, or femininity and masculinity combined; blue for masculinity; white for nonbinary or neutral; and black for any gender identity that does not fall under traditional descriptions.

GENDERQUEER FLAG, by Marilyn Roxie, **2011:** Lavender for androgyny, or femininity and masculinity combined; white for nonbinary or neutral; green, the inverse of lavender, for third gender, or any other gender. Similar and simplified version of the Genderfluid Flag.

POLYSEXUAL FLAG, by Samlin, Tumblr user, **2012:** Pink for attraction to female-identifying people, green for nonbinary and neutral-identifying people, and blue for male-identifying people.

FEMME/LIPSTICK LESBIAN FLAG, by anonymous lesbian blogger, **2010:** Designed as a flag for femme-identifying lesbians and not lesbians as a whole, although some lesbians who do not identify as femme or lipstick have complained that this flag isn't inclusive.

LESBIAN PRIDE FLAG, by Sean Campbell, **1999:** Lavender for its synonymousness with the LGBTQ+ community, black triangle to represent the triangle symbol used to identify queers in Nazi times, and a labrys to represent matriarchal power.

POLYAMORY FLAG, by Jim Evans, **1995:** The pi symbol is used as a discreet code for "polyamory," with the idea that they both start with the letter "p." Also, Evans said that the pi symbol was one of the few available characters on computers at the time of the flag's conception.

INTERSEX FLAG, by Morgan Carpenter of Intersex International Australia, **2013:** Features the nongendered colors of yellow and purple; the circle symbolizes the wholeness, completeness, and potentiality of intersex people.

PANSEXUAL FLAG, 2010: Pink symbolizes attraction to female-identifying people, yellow symbolizes attraction to nonbinary and neutral-identifying people, and blue symbolizes attraction to male-identifying people.

ASEXUAL FLAG, by Asexual Visibility and Education Network, **2010:** Black for asexuality, gray for the "gray" area between sexual and asexual, white for non-asexual partners and allies, and purple for community.

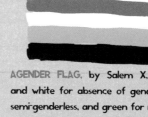

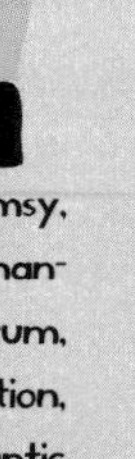

AROMANTIC FLAG, by cameronwhimsy, Tumblr user, **2014:** Dark green for aromanticism, light green for aromantic spectrum, white for platonic and aesthetic attraction, gray for gray-romantic and demiromantic people, and black for the sexuality spectrum.

AGENDER FLAG, by Salem X, **2014:** Black and white for absence of gender, gray for semi-genderless, and green for nonbinary, as green is the inverse of purple, which is heavily saturated with ties to gender identity.

NONBINARY FLAG, by Kye Rowan, **2014:** Designed for nonbinary people who do not really identify with traditional gender roles. Yellow for people's genders that exist outside the binary; white for people with many or all genders; purple for androgyny, or a mix of female and male gender; and black for people who do not identify with any gender, or being agender.

STRAIGHT ALLY FLAG, late **2000s:** Rainbow for LGBTQ+ community, black and white for heterosexual and cisgender people, "A" shape to represent the word "ally," designed as a symbol for allies of the LGBTQ+ community.

BISEXUAL FLAG, by Michael Page, **1998:** Pink for attraction to female-identifying people, purple for attraction to both female-identifying and male-identifying people, blue for attraction to male-identifying people.

TRANSGENDER FLAG, by Monica Helms, **1999:** Blue for boys, pink for girls, and white for the in between, neutral, or nonbinary. Because of its symmetrical orientation, no matter which way the flag is hung, it is always correct, a connection that Helms says is reflective of transitioning in general: no matter which path you are on, you are never wrong. It was first flown at a pride parade in Phoenix, Arizona, in **2000**.

Coming Out

Coming out is acknowledging your queer differences from the heteronormative way of life, and it's very different for everyone. Some people know from early childhood about their sexuality and identity and it comes naturally, while others struggle with acceptance of themselves and of other people. There are even some people who don't realize they are not heterosexual or don't identify as their biological gender until much later in life! For example, Ash didn't realize that she was queer until she was nineteen years old, and Chess, on the other hand, knew since childhood (but didn't come out until much later)! Every single person's story is different. Whether you are someone who is awaiting the right moment to come out (spoiler: just like all the crazy things in life, there is never really a "perfect" time) to a friend or a parent, or even if you're a curious bystander who's wondering "What's the big deal about coming out?," here are some guidelines for when it's time for the big reveal.

Simply put, coming out is essentially declaring that you are different from seemingly everyone around you. Unfortunately, the way that a majority of society perceives the LGBTQ+ community can make coming out a difficult and negative experience. Coming out *should* be as easy as telling everyone that you like pizza more than sushi, or that you prefer blue to green. But it's not that easy when it comes to who you love and what gender you identify with, although as each day passes, more and more people are finding the courage to live life outside the closet and are contributing to the normalization of living openly. Have you ever wondered why straight people don't come out? It's because we live in a world where good ol'-fashioned straight couples are the norm. But someday, hopefully, in the words of Harvey Milk, all closet doors will be destroyed, and the pain and uneasiness of coming out will no longer be an issue for the LGBTQ+ community.

Why Is It Called "Coming Out" or "Coming Out of the Closet"?

There is not an exact clear time when the phrase "coming out of the closet" or "in the closet" was first used, but it seems likely to have been sometime after the 1960s. The closet part is said to be a riff on having skeletons in the closet. In other words, keeping a shameful secret!

Coming Out Dos and Don'ts

What's the most important thing when someone you know comes out? Support, support, support. If there's one thing we've all experienced in the trials and tribulations of life, it's feeling alone, like you're the only one, no matter what the situation might be. We've all been there, and do you remember how it feels? IT FEELS BAD. So when someone you know comes out, instead of condemning them based on your beliefs or telling them they are wrong or disturbed, or even the classic "Where did I go wrong raising you?," do the OPPOSITE of bad things and give them SUPPORT.

DON'T:

- tell them they're confused
- tell them it's just a phase
- ask them where you went wrong raising them
- disown them
- kick them out of the house
- sign them up for conversion therapy

DO:

- respect new pronouns or new chosen name
- join a support group if you don't know how to handle this news
- hang out with other LGBTQ+ parents and allies
- be supportive where you can
- ask questions
- try to have a mind-set open to learning and listening

Questions That Are Okay and Not Okay to Ask

First of all, we hope that this book as a whole will answer many of your questions about the LGBTQ+ community, the inner workings of it, and what makes it such a great, amazing, diverse rainbow of people! With that being said, there are always going to be questions that we miss, questions that we get wrong, and questions that are left unanswered. Here are a few examples of questions that LGBTQ+ people get asked often!

Which one of you is the man in the relationship? Let's get one thing straight: this question is offensive and closed-minded because it's the twenty-first century and you can love whoever the f*ck you want. The combination of one cisgender hetero woman and one cisgender hetero man is not the only way to have a valid romantic relationship. Although this is often asked of lesbian couples, or even nonbinary couples, this question is based on the simple idea that a "correct" couple should be a man and a woman. Yes, some people may have more butch or androgynous qualities while some are very femme, but this in no way means that either is the "man" in the relationship if neither identify exclusively as male. It's simple math, everyone! If there are no male-identifiers in the relationship, then neither is the man in the relationship.

Where did I go wrong raising you? This question is hurtful and implies that the person coming out is bad. The question alone is punishment; the mere shame and resentment that radiates off it is harmful to anyone's delicate being. There is nothing wrong with being gay, trans, nonbinary, or anything other than straight, and it is not a choice by any means. Some may argue that *acting on it* is a choice, and in a sense it is, but it's not a reason to condemn someone if you don't "believe in gay." If you think that the way you raised your child made them gay, you're wrong. If anything, all of those beautiful souls out there who are forced to choose to be someone they're not because of the heteronormative and gender binaries that are pushed onto them by either unaccepting or unknowing parents are the ones who have been raised wrong. The only thing that matters from this point on is continuing to love your child unconditionally and supporting them no matter what their sexual orientation or gender identity is.

When did you know? If you are genuinely interested in the person who is coming out, this is a great question to ask.

How can I support you? This question helps whoever came out to you feel like they have a trusted ally in you, and like they can rely on you when times are tough. They may or may not have an immediate response on how they'd like to be supported, or how they need you, but it's helpful to know that someone is there when the occasion arises.

The Bad Parts About Coming Out

Not everyone gets to have a smooth coming-out story. Some are better than others, some are absolutely traumatizing, some people are lucky to have a supporting family and have no problems at all. Unfortunately, there are thousands of LGBTQ+ youth that are thrown out of their homes or abused, or who run away because of the rejection of their queerness. Almost half of the homeless youth population identify as part of the LGBTQ+ community! Rejection of one's sexual orientation or gender identity by loved ones can be absolutely debilitating, and a lot of the time results in homelessness and even suicide. The most important thing that you can do for someone coming out is to respect their decision, even if it is someone of a younger age. You don't agree that *you're* the one in the wrong for not wanting to support and love this person unconditionally, no matter how they need to live their life? Maybe you're the one that needs to make some changes.

Do You Have to Come Out?

Coming out is not mandatory by any means. Lots of people have relationships or romantic affairs with people of the same gender, but do not consider themselves queer or bisexual. Some people are happy not sharing their personal lives with the public, or just aren't in a situation where they are ready to. Coming out is a personal choice, and there is a lot to consider when you come out. It sucks that we are still living in a world where being queer has a negative stigma, but the more people who come out, the more that stigma washes away. But don't ever feel pressured to come out, especially if you're not ready! Finding yourself and understanding your own personal quirks and qualities sometimes take time.

Outing People: Hard No

What is outing someone and why is it wrong? Outing someone is revealing a person's sexual orientation or gender identity without their consent. Outing someone is not something that anyone should ever do. If they're not out yet, that's their choice. It is not your job to make public the secrets of someone else's life, no matter what the subject. When you out someone who isn't ready, it could destroy their relationships, their professional life, and their trust in you (obviously). There's a reason they haven't shared with the world yet, so respect that. It's not your secret to share.

THEY/THEM

When Is the Right Time to Come Out?

Surprise! There will never be a right time to come out. Coming out can be the hardest thing or the easiest thing, depending on your situation. You just have to decide if you want to come out in the first place and if you feel ready. If you are afraid of coming out due to fear of rejection, just know that you are not alone. So many LGBTQ+ people have dealt, will deal, and are currently dealing with rejection on a daily basis, so always remember: you're not the only one. Befriending other queers in the community is always a good idea so you can count on having a support system in place if things go horribly wrong. Community is everything.

How Do You Come Out?

Coming out can happen however you want it to (unless someone outs you, which is TOTALLY RUDE!). You can tell people one by one, you can gather everyone together and make an announcement, you can send an e-mail, you can write a letter, you can write it on a cake, you can post it on Instagram . . . the options are truly endless. And when you come out, you don't have to tell EVERYONE you know; you can take it slow and only tell people who you think need to or should know. Do what is comfortable for you, because at the end of the day, YOU are in control of your life.

Will Coming Out Make Me Happier?

Listen, coming out is not always easy, and there most likely will be tears. We'll tell you from firsthand experience that sometimes it feels like it's not going to get better, in terms of acceptance. Sometimes it will but sometimes it won't. But in general, being liberated feels really great, and in a lot of cases, you will be happier because you won't have to hide who you truly are anymore and can find some people to smooch if you want.

How Do I Come Out as Trans/Genderqueer?

Coming out as a different gender can be really hard because a lot of people don't have the brain capacity to imagine anything outside of traditional heteronormative ways of life. When you come out as trans or genderqueer, you can start with providing your new pronouns and, if you want, your new chosen name.

PRIDE BUTTONS

Pinbacks started showing up at the end of the nineteenth century for promoting political campaigns, but became a huge trend for the LGBTQ+ community in more recent years. Picked up by activists, they were an easy way to publicly voice opinions, beliefs, and sexual orientation. They became extremely important to the LGBTQ+ community, as they were a simple and effective way to get a message across. Not only do buttons make statements of something you support, they can be a way to let other queers around you know that they are not the only queer in the room. But remember, showing your true colors was not always as accepted as it is today. Wearing pride buttons showed (and still shows) that individuals had the courage to display their true selves.

CHOSEN FAMILY

Having a chosen family in the queer community is, a lot of the time, a necessity. A chosen family is comprised of the people you choose to surround yourself with, people who love you like you are family, especially in the absence of a supportive biological family. This is crucial in the queer community because when you're living openly as queer, sometimes it's easy to feel like you're the only one, especially after dealing with rejection and hate. Having a strong and supportive circle of queer friends and allies is key for growing and being happy! When our biological families can't love us in the ways we need them to, we turn to our chosen family.

The concept of having a chosen family has been around for a long time, especially in cases of homeless LGBTQ+ members. Getting kicked to the curb by your biological family is definitely a 0 on the fun scale and one of the biggest rejections anyone can face in their lifetime. Even in the 1980s and '90s, when ball culture began to blow up, house mothers and fathers would take in homeless and rejected LGBTQ+ people with nowhere to go and provide for them. Think of Marsha P. Johnson and Sylvia Rivera's STAR House as a chosen family, because that's exactly what it was. Cultivating relationships, supporting one another, and helping each other grow as the amazing queer people you were meant to become while sometimes living under the same roof, or just being close to your queer peers, is what having a chosen family is all about.

Dating

Dating is a very natural part of life. It's kind of like sampling ice cream flavors with those cute little wooden spoons before finding one you *really* like and want to commit to. It's a way to explore different types of people and types of relationships, all leading to the discovery of what *you* like. It can be fun, it can be heartbreaking, and it can be not for you! News flash: queer dating has its similarities to heterosexual dating, obviously, like having crushes, feeling nervous, or, if you are asexual, not feeling a need to date at all.

When it comes to queer dating, it's all about exploration. Owning your sexuality is so important, and through meeting people and developing romantic relationships, you can maybe someday achieve ultimate self-satisfaction despite what society has to say. Unless it's the queer society—then we say get it, queen. For a very long time, before the gay rights movement really started to take off, dating in public was hard. Hate crimes happened more often (although it's tragic that they are still happening today . . .) to couples in public, people in drag, exposed queers, and the whole shebang. People got fired for their sexuality and faced discrimination, they were excommunicated by families and churches, the list goes on. But this ties into the dating world—if you wanted to meet other LGBTQ+ folks and have a good time back in the day, well, you had to do it in secret. Secret codes, discreet gay bar guides, classified ads, and organizations that were kept on the down low were practically your only ways to meet the big gay person of your dreams. Fast forward to 2020 and see how it's changed: queer people can not only date in public a lot more comfortably now, but there are even apps and websites made *specifically* for the queer community around dating and meeting other queers! And gay bars are poppin' like crazy—so poppin' that the clientele isn't even limited to queers anymore. Parts of society have welcomed the LGBTQ+ community with open arms, embracing their existence. And it's amazing.

SAFE SEX

Typically, when sex education is taught in schools (if at all!), the focus is on cisgender heterosexual intercourse, with a main focus on pregnancy prevention and reducing the risk of sexually transmitted infections (STIs). This created a big problem for the LGBTQ+ population—programs that typically do not acknowledge changing gender identities and sexual behaviors outside of the "norm" do not prepare people to have safe sexual interactions. These antiquated resources often refer to "men" and "women" to simply mean "men" have penises and "women" have vaginas, and they go together. This does not acknowledge that body parts do not define a person's gender, and a penis and vagina are not necessarily men's and women's body parts. Additionally, a person's gender identity simply refers to the internal state of being a male, female, in between, or neither and can include gender expression and gender roles. It is different from sex, which a medical professional assigns at birth based upon genitals. Sexual orientation also has nothing to do with gender identity, and only has to do with who the person is attracted to.

Sexual consent is important in every sexual encounter, regardless of gender identity, sexuality, or relationship status. Checking in with your sexual partner before, during, and after sexual activity can encourage a healthy environment where sex can remain positive. Consent can come in many forms. Verbal consent is an explicit interaction in which both parties agree to an activity by talking about it. This is different from implied consent, which is given through actions or body language. This is a gray area, as body language and actions are very subjective and can be interpreted differently based upon someone's personality or many other factors, such as drugs or alcohol. It's best to get verbal consent as well, especially with a new partner, and to talk to your partner about ways in which they imply consent. Contractual consent involves a written contract, and can be extremely useful to people engaging in sex work.

STIs can be contracted during sexual activity. The Centers for Disease Control and Prevention says that nearly twenty million STIs are contracted per year, and half of those cases are in young people. A sexually transmitted infection is passed through sexual contact, such as vaginal, anal, or oral sex; or other contact with fluids like blood or semen. Many STIs do not show symptoms, so it is important to get tested. Most STIs are easily treated bacterial or viral infections. To prevent STIs, in addition to frequent testing it is important to use condoms, dams, PrEP, and/or vaccinations.

One of the main forms of protection is preventive care—knowing your own sexual health and STI status is important. Establishing a relationship with a reliable health care provider who makes you feel safe with your gender identity and sexual practices is also key, as this creates an open space for dialogue. Talking about STIs and sexual histories with partners is also important to practice—this includes informing new partners of any current STIs and asking new partners when they last got tested. Keep in mind, STIs are extremely common and are not a basis for shame or embarrassment; however, it is your responsibility to share this status with past partners who may have been exposed, and with current partners. Safe sex is another way of practicing self-care, and should not be glossed over.

DOMESTIC PARTNERSHIPS & Civil Unions

Before same-sex marriage was made fully legal in the U.S. in 2015, domestic partnerships and civil unions were basically like "knockoff" marriages for queer couples, definitely a "separate but equal" vibe. Although neither of these formal relationship statuses were created exclusively for same-sex couples, they have been a very important step along the way for actual same-sex marriage. Generally speaking, these alternatives to marriage give the two people in the relationship certain benefits, rights, and other protections, but not the whole package that comes with marriage. Domestic partnerships offer limited protections depending on your city or state, civil unions offer state-level protections, and marriages offer federal-level protections. Now remember, not everyone wants to be married, so it's nice that there are some non-marriage options out there! Each option involves a bunch of boring legal details, so we'll just cover the basics for now if you're thinking of taking it to the next level soon! Also, to make this topic less boring to read, these will be described as if they are cell phone plans.

Domestic Partnership, Silver Plan—Domestic partnerships are the most basic legal relationship plan. Rights, protections, benefits, and other details depend on the city or state you apply in. This plan does not require a witness, allowing the option of *Secret Romance* if desired by the customer. Guaranteed benefits: inheritance of a partner's estate after their death and hospital visitation rights. Service may be cut off if you enter an area your plan doesn't cover. Must live together at the same address in order to qualify. DISCLAIMER: opposite-sex couples wishing to seek a domestic partnership plan in the state of California must have at least one member over the age of sixty-two.

Civil Union, Gold Plan—Civil unions are for customers looking for more perks than what the domestic partnership plan has to offer, but fewer benefits than marriage. Included is pretty much everything the domestic partnership plan covers, plus more! With this plan, you and your partner will get protections at a state level. Some customers even say that it's close enough to marriage, so there ya go! Great for anyone queer wanting to be legally married before the year **2015**. DISCLAIMER: not all states recognize civil unions.

Marriage, Diamond Plan—Marriage includes everything you ever dreamed of: federal recognition and benefits galore. Oh, and perks for joint-filing your taxes as well. DISCLAIMER: terminating this plan has the potential to cost you hundreds, if not thousands, of dollars.

surrogate mother
CONTRACT
Adoption Papers!

Starting a family for any type of queer couple can be quite tricky, especially for those who physically don't have the required parts, resources, or desire to even get pregnant. Obtaining a baby can be a difficult journey, but it can also be an easy one depending on your situation. The process is different for every single person.

ADOPTION Adoption is an option for families in which neither partner wants to or is able to carry a child. Adoption can be pricey and take a very long time to complete. Just ballpark, it costs, like, thirty thousand dollars on average to adopt a child. If anyone reading this has an influence over the adoption business, can that someone please figure out a cheaper and easier way to adopt? Thirty thousand dollars is an outrageous number: WHAT, you have to be rich to have a baby if your anatomy doesn't allow it? I'm talking for all the cis heterosexual people out here, too, by the way. K, thanks.

FREEZE EGGS!
FIND SURROGATE!

DONOR Some couples find a sperm donor, either someone close to them or a donor from a sperm bank. Sperm can be inserted into the egg of the partner who wishes to carry the child, or even into the egg of a surrogate mother. This is most often associated with the classic turkey baster method.

IN VITRO In vitro fertilization is when the egg is extracted from a partner's or donor's body, fertilized with donor sperm manually in a petri dish, and then inserted into the uterus of the person who will be carrying the child. This option is also pricey and has a lower success rate.

SURROGATE A surrogate is a person you can hire to carry a child for you. With a surrogate, you have the ability to choose the sperm donor. It is common to pay surrogate mothers a buttload of cash because carrying a baby for nine months is a lot to ask. Also, with this option, the couple hiring the surrogate will typically pay for hospital and doctor visits, medicine and supplements, and anything really that has to do with the comfort of the surrogate carrying their baby.

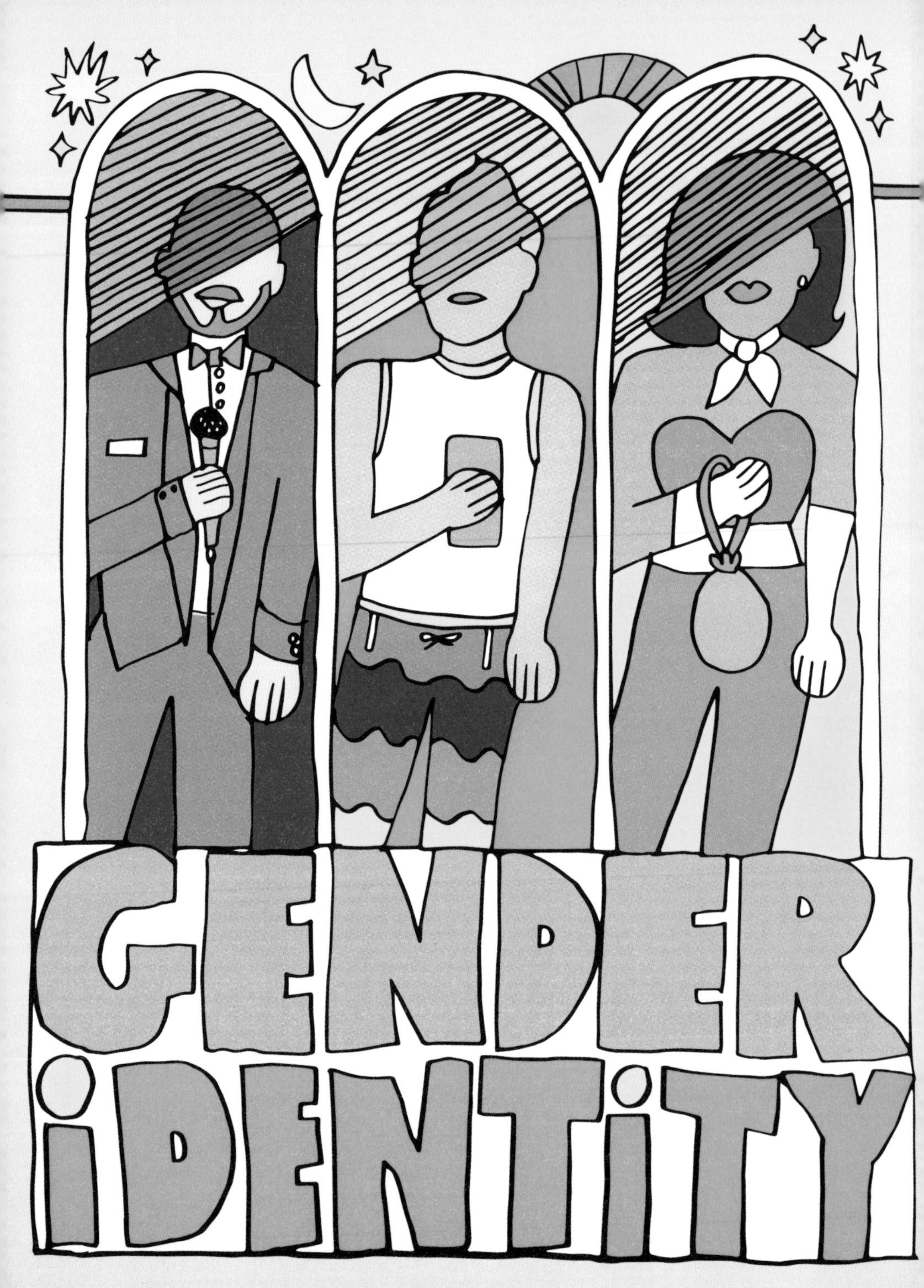
GENDER
iDENTiTY

Below are some of the terms that are most commonly used for gender identity, with thanks to the Hetrick-Martin Institute and the Lurie Children's Hospital for the definitions. Gender identity does not go hand in hand with one's sexual or romantic feelings; it simply expresses a person's deep sense of being male, female, neither, both, or other. Gender is so wrapped up in societal norms that often it can be a complex, painful, and dysphoric part of someone's life.

Gender Gender is the state of presenting "masculine" or "feminine" traits. The problem with gender is that it forces individuals to conform to societal standards. For example, someone may gender a blue toy truck by saying it's a boy's toy, and a girl who is interested in the truck could be made to feel shamed or "wrong." Similarly, a boy could be made to feel incorrect for liking a pink doll, which society dictates is a girl's toy. Gender is a spectrum, and is often tied into capitalist and social constructs.

Sex Sex refers to the sexual organs that one has at birth. A person's body may have been born with male, female, or intersex genitalia, but that does not necessarily define what gender they identify with or anything else about them.

Cisgender A cisgender person is someone whose gender identity is the same as their sex assigned at birth. This does not indicate their gender expression, sexual orientation, anatomy, or perception.

Sex Assigned at Birth The assignment or classification of people as male, female, or intersex assigned at birth based upon physical anatomy. This sex often does not reflect a person's gender expression or sexuality.

Genderfluid A genderfluid person has a changing or "fluid" gender identity.

Trans Woman/Trans Man "Trans woman" often describes someone who was assigned male at birth and identifies as a woman, while a "trans man" is someone who was assigned female at birth and identifies as a man. They may or may not self-identify as transgender.

Personal Gender Pronoun She/he/they/ze/xe or any pronoun that one prefers when not using their name.

Transgender A transgender person is someone whose gender identity differs from the sex they were assigned at birth. Identifying as transgender does not define a person's gender expression, hormonal makeup, or physical anatomy.

Nonbinary An umbrella term for all genders aside from male/female. Not all nonbinary people identify as transgender, and this term is often used to describe the aesthetic and expression of a cisgender or transgender person. Many nonbinary people choose to use a nonbinary pronoun, such as they or xe.

Gender Expression The physical appearance of a person, which may or may not align with their gender identity.

Agender This describes people who do not have a gender or feel that they have a neutral gender.

Genderqueer An identity that can be used by people who do not identify within the gender binary and may see themselves as outside or in the middle of the gender binary. Many who identify as genderqueer identify with genderqueer as an aesthetic, and not everyone who identifies as genderqueer is nonbinary or transgender.

Gender-Affirming Surgery Surgical alteration to reflect someone's gender identity. Most people associate this with the trans community, however, only a small minority of trans people choose to or can afford to have gender-affirming surgery.

Sexual Orientation A person's physical, romantic, emotional, or other form of attraction to others.

Queer Matchbooks

Back in the day, smoking indoors was a thing. Naturally, businesses took the opportunity to supply matchbooks to patrons with their info, almost like multifunctional business cards. Not only were the matchbooks for lending someone a light, but they often doubled as a safe place to take down someone special's phone number: as you can probably recall, cell phones weren't around yet! Matchbooks are all we have left of some of the gay bars and establishments of the past. Before the Internet, it was considerably more difficult to find information about gay businesses. Your only means were word of mouth and minimal advertising, especially since being out in the open was a rocky thing back then. Ephemera like matchbooks, menus, pinbacks, flyers, and brochures can tell you so much about a place, even if they're small in size.

TRANSITIONING

Transitioning can be a big part of a trans person's story. However, it's important to know that a transition does not always mean gender-affirming surgery. In fact, only a small population of the trans community has gender-affirming surgery, either due to not wanting it, not being able to afford it, or other reasons that they don't really need to share with you! A transition can mean much more than having surgery—as you should have previously learned in this book, physical body parts do not mean much of anything in the gender spectrum.

Transitioning is simply the process of changing how you are perceived by others so that you can express the gender that you feel on the inside. A trans person's journey does not have to be male to female or female to male, but can also fall anywhere in between. Transitioning just has to do with matching how you feel on the inside to how you are perceived on the outside. It can mean undergoing medical treatment, or it can mean just changing your name or appearance. Many trans people go through a social transition. This can include coming out, changing pronouns, changing your name, or changing your appearance.

A medical transition does not only mean gender-affirming surgery but can also be hormone therapy in order to create more masculine or feminine characteristics. For trans men, medically transitioning can include top surgery (removal of breast tissue to create a more masculine look to the chest), a hysterectomy, construction of a penis, and/or hormone therapy to make the clitoris grow larger. For trans women, medical transitions can include breast augmentation, facial feminization surgery, laser hair removal, creation of a vagina, removal of testes, and/or hormone therapy.

Not everyone who is transgender or genderqueer transitions. For some, it may not be safe to even socially transition. Some may not want to or feel the need to. Some may transition socially but never transition medically. Regardless of how "far" someone has transitioned, their gender identity should be respected no matter what.

"Transitioning just has to do with matching how you feel on the inside to how you are perceived on the outside."

DRAG

Most people have witnessed the beautifully made-up, fierce, and super theatrical personas of drag queens. Drag culture is still very much alive and well, with drag shows across the world, YouTube stars, and more and more representation on mainstream media—you'd be hard-pressed to find someone who doesn't know and love RuPaul. However, this isn't new. Drag has a long history, dating back centuries to when men dressed as women as a part of common theater culture, and a tumultuous relationship with the LGBTQ+ community. Drag was buried in underground clubs and bars and kept on the down low, while drag queens often would be denied entry into gay bars.

Now, simply cross-dressing goes back centuries and centuries. Indigenous groups frequently used cross-dressing for religious ceremonies, and the popular seventeenth-century Japanese Kabuki theater exclusively featured men cross-dressing and speaking in high falsetto voices. Drag has always had its roots in the theatrical, the drama, and the performance! Nowadays, drag (and really anything "effeminate") and homosexuality are almost seen as going hand in hand, but back then, this expression of flamboyance was completely separate from homosexuality. The role of drag at that time was, actually, to reinforce strict gender roles: it was undignified for women to be seen putting on such a show of emotion.

The link between drag culture and the gay community didn't occur until centuries later, in the 1930s, when scientists studying sex began speaking about homosexuality and the third sex, and drag queens began performing in back-alley clubs and bars (which, let's not forget, were illegal at the time). Drag personas developed quickly and soon became a central part of the experimental theater scene in New York City. Drag queens embraced the theatrical and were not afraid to go over the top, often relying on humor to draw an audience. And it worked! The drag scene grew and queens became more and more confident. In 2009, *RuPaul's Drag Race* premiered and brought drag even more into the mainstream.

HOMOPHOBIA

Homophobia *irrational fear of, aversion to, or discrimination against homosexuality or homosexuals*

"Homophobia" was first used in print in 1969, though the concept of homophobia existed way before then. The year 1969 is often said to mark the beginning of the gay liberation movement, usually associated with the Stonewall riots and various other protests and demonstrations leading up to that point. Since the beginning of the 1900s and earlier, people in the gay community, along with other minority groups, have been underdogs when it came to being treated equally and with respect. Homophobia stems from several things. The church's condemnation of homosexual behavior had a big impact on presenting the idea that gay people were "sexually deviant"; in other words, their sexuality strayed from the Bible's concerns about reproductive activity, and the Bible called it an "abomination, punishable by death." Because how can a woman have a baby without having sex with a man? How can a child have two fathers? This misconception that gays were sexual deviants continued on to create this incorrect representation of the gay community: that homosexuals are obsessed with sex. Psychologists, influenced by the church's aversion to gays, eventually deemed homosexuality a perversion and classified it as a mental illness. People became afraid of the gays, basically fearing nonconsensual sexual acts (of the rape sort) from the gay community upon heterosexual people, only feeding into the negativity that comes with being associated with mental illness and perversion.

How to Identify a Homophobe

Don't confuse someone who is actually a classic homophobic gay-hater for someone who is just influenced by the anti-gay bias that society has been pounding into our brains since birth and doesn't know that gay people have feelings, too. Just because someone is uneducated or might have made a homophobic comment in passing doesn't necessarily mean they are homophobic; it could mean that they just don't know that what they said was homophobic or have never been called out on it. Consideration for other people's lives and feelings is something that EVERYONE struggles with. Some people have it in them to change, although it is devastating when we find out that the people we love have no desire to eliminate hate from their lives. The hate culture that was accepted back in the day, and unfortunately still is in many areas, has made it seem okay to slur the gay community and make jokes at their expense. If you are a member of the LGBTQ+ community, it is your duty to help shed light on *why* stuff like this is not okay. A little education and a willingness to share your perspective can be helpful in changing the negative rhetoric that has been attached to the LGBTQ+ community since the beginning.

Now, real, clear-as-day, full-on homophobes are the types that claim, "I love you but I don't approve of your lifestyle" or "You will not live in this house as long as you're gay." This also extends to people who use derogatory terms like "faggot," "tranny," and the like, out of spite or pure hatred. Homophobes can't always be changed, and don't be too hard on yourself if you feel like you can't win after being put down. It really blows to be rejected by family or friends, but if you experience this type of hate in your life, know that we all go through it in one way or another.

HOW TO HANDLE HOMOPHOBES

1. Give them this book.
2. Show them that you are a human being and it's the twenty-first century and being not "normal" is the new normal, and that hate and bigotry are so fifty years ago.
3. Try gently educating them about the LGBTQ+ community.
4. Try (key word: try! It's hard) not to take it personally. Find a safe space to talk with others about dealing with the pain of homophobia, and know that your feelings are normal.
5. If it's safe, intervene when someone is speaking hatefully against the community. If you feel comfortable, direct them toward resources (articles, blogs, etc.) that can help educate them.
6. Remember that you are a person who loves or feels attraction to another person. You are a normal person with hopes, dreams, and desires.

HOMOPHOBIA AND RELIGION

Unfortunately, many homeless LGBTQ+ youth come from families with strong religious backgrounds. It is devastating the number of homeless youth who identify as LGBTQ+: a whopping 40 percent. Homophobia in religious groups has also resulted in the creation of conversion camps and conversion therapy, instilling an unnecessary fear of hell in the hearts and minds of LGBTQ+ people and scaring queer people into living lives they do not want in order to make other people happy, such as marrying a person of the opposite sex. However, today there are many denominations that are openly welcoming of LGBTQ+ people, including the Presbyterian Church (USA), the Episcopal Church, the United Church of Christ, Reform Judaism, and Islamic Modernism, all of which ordain gay ministers and rabbis, perform gay marriages, and do not discriminate against anyone.

RELIGION & BEING GAY: CAN I BE LGBTQ+ AND RELIGIOUS?

Religion surrounds many families as a form of community and guidance. However, religion has also been used as a weapon to deny progress and to justify homophobia. The relationship, therefore, between the queer community and religion is complicated. Many fundamentalist views of religion treat the LGBTQ+ community harshly and use religion as a backdrop for their hatred; while others, like Reform Judaism and Episcopalianism, are supportive and accepting of LGBTQ+ members. In fact, Chess's mom is a rabbi and very supportive of Ash and Chess. Hi, Mom! The fact of the matter is, if you are religious, want to become religious, or want to be less religious, that's all fine. You can be religious and be LGBTQ+. You can find churches, synagogues, mosques, temples, and so on that will accept you; there are so many denominations that are openly welcoming of LGBTQ+ people such as the Presbyterian Church (USA), the Episcopal Church, the United Church of Christ, Reform Judaism, and Islamic Modernism, which all ordain gay ministers and rabbis, perform gay marriages, and do not discriminate against anyone. You can find affirming places of worship or resources via Gay Church's website, PFLAG, the Institute for Welcoming Resources, Equally Blessed, Queer Jihad, Keshet, and many more. You are not alone.

CONVERSION THERAPY

Quite often targeted at minors under eighteen, conversion therapy is most commonly associated with Christian churches. It is a harmful practice aimed to change, or "cure," the sexual orientation or gender identity of a person who does not identify as heterosexual or cisgender. This practice is banned in many states, though it is still going on somewhere every day. Currently, laws are on the table to ban conversion therapy for minors because many believe that it should be the person in question's decision to seek out help if they feel that they need or want it once they come of age (eighteen). Many people who have gone through conversion therapy have claimed that it didn't work (what a surprise!) and have gone on to share testimonies on the Internet, through memoirs, through movies, and through word of mouth. Some, though, didn't make it out alive. Being exposed to such unethical and mentally scarring practices has resulted in suicides due to imposed shame and guilt.

Although conversion therapy is often forced upon kids, some adults willingly participate in it as well. There have been cases where even exorcisms have been performed to "get the gay demon out." It didn't help that the APA deemed being gay a mental illness in the fifties, leading to more extreme treatments such as electroshock therapy and conversion therapy. Many argue that God wouldn't make someone gay and that having gay feelings and attractions is a choice, which is the basis on which the concept of conversion therapy thrives. In a way, organizations providing conversion therapy are nothing more than just people pushing gays into a corner and threatening eternal hell and unhappiness upon them unless they get straight real quick!

HATE GROUPS

What is a hate group? A hate group is a group of like-minded people who advocate for hostility and hatred toward a specific category of people who have characteristics or practices that the group doesn't agree with. This can be anything from race to religion, gender identity, sexual orientation, or ethnicity. For example, one of the most widely known hate groups out there is the Ku Klux Klan, a hate group that for whatever garbage reason think that only white people should exist and rule the world. I'm cringing even writing about this topic. Hate groups exist everywhere today, and in every form imaginable, which is a total bummer, considering that they are only promoting and fueling unwarranted hate, and let me tell you, the world does not need more of that. Luckily there are organizations like the Southern Poverty Law Center that monitor the activities and whereabouts of hate groups, and news pertaining to human rights issues. Many of the organizations classified as LGBTQ+ hate groups today strongly express disdain for and oppose expanding LGBTQ+ rights, essentially trying to keep queer folks as second-class citizens, with the goal of erasing them from existence. If you have ever dealt with homophobia, that is just a taste of what hate groups against the queer community stand for.

THE GAY GENE AND SEXUAL FLUIDITY

The "gay gene" theory was first presented as a possible scientific explanation for homosexual behavior in men in 1993 by geneticist Dean Hamer, specifically through a finding of a genetic variation on the X chromosome that was thought to correlate with a person's sexual orientation. But this theory was never fully proved, and the actual scientific explanation of why people are attracted to the same sex is still in question. While there are still studies being conducted to get down to the bottom of this gay business, it is still basically unknown what makes a person gay, or queer, or trans, or fluid. Sexual orientation can be ever-changing over the course of a lifetime. The Kinsey scale is a direct example of sexual fluidity. You may fall into one number on the chart right now, but where will you be in ten years? Your sexual identity doesn't have to be one thing forever, and luckily we are now living in a day and age where being persecuted for "forbidden love" isn't *as* common as it used to be (although, unfortunately, it still happens . . .). The concept of sexual fluidity means that love is love and you can love anyone, no matter what their gender. And if there really is a gene out there that makes you feel gay things, it is probably rainbow colored and glittery.

ACKNOWLEDGMENTS

We want to thank Meg Thompson, our literary agent who found us on the internet. She is super cool and has been probably the best thing that happened in our lives, and this book would have never existed without her.

Thank you to our editor, Emma Brodie, who helped us every step of the way and made our dreams come true with the most rainbow book ever.

Thanks to our wonderful team at Morrow Gift, whom we appreciate so much for all the work that was put in to make this book: Liate Stehlik, Ben Steinberg, Cassie Jones, Leah Carlson-Stanisic, Kyle O'Brien, Yeon Kim, Mumtaz Mustafa, Susan Kosko, Greg Villepique, Shelby Peak, and Andrew Gibeley.

Thanks to Michael C. Oliveira at ONE Archives in Los Angeles and Kelsi Evans at the GLBT Historical Society in San Francisco for helping us with our research.

Thanks to everyone who sent in photos to be drawn into the book. We are so happy that we had the opportunity to represent real actual queer people in this book about queer things!

And thanks to our animals, Boomer, Pepper, and Mafia, for being soft and cuddly when we needed something to hold, and to our friends who gave us support and many nice compliments along the way.

BIBLIOGRAPHY

Abrams, Mere. "LGBTQIA Safe Sex Guide." Healthline. www.healthline.com/health/lgbtqia-safe-sex-guide.

"Activism Before Stonewall." NYC LGBT Historic Sites Project. www.nyclgbtsites.org/theme/activism-before-stonewall/.

Ben, Lisa. "Vice Versa." *Vice Versa* 1, no. 2 (1947). queermusicheritage.com/viceversa2.html.

Cisneros, Lisa. "Thirty Years of AIDS." UCSF. March 23, 2012. www.ucsf.edu/news/2011/06/104134/thirty-years-aids-timeline-epidemic.

Clews, Colin. "1984. Wigstock." Gay in the 80s, March 11, 2013. www.gayinthe80s.com/2013/03/1984-wigstock/.

Fishberger, Jeffrey, Phoenix Schneider, and Henry Ng. *Coming Out as You*. The Trevor Project. 2017. www.thetrevorproject.org/wp-content/uploads/2017/09/ComingOutAsYou.pdf.

Gonzalez, Nora. "How Did the Rainbow Flag Become a Symbol of LGBTQ Pride?" *Encyclopaedia Britannica*. www.britannica.com/story/how-did-the-rainbow-flag-become-a-symbol-of-lgbt-pride.

"History of HIV and AIDS Overview." Avert. October 10, 2019. www.avert.org/professionals/history-hiv-aids/overview.

Iovannone, Jeffry J. "Leslie Feinberg." Queer History For the People. June 23, 2018. medium.com/queer-history-for-the-people/leslie-feinberg-transgender-warrior-fcb1bcaf15b2.

Iovannone, Jeffry J. "Rita Mae Brown." Queer History For the People. June 4, 2018. medium.com/queer-history-for-the-people/rita-mae-brown-lavender-menace-759dd376b6bc.

Katz, Jonathan. *Gay American History*. New York: Meridian, 1992.

"The Kinsey Scale." Kinsey Institute. kinseyinstitute.org/research/publications/kinsey-scale.php.

Kohler, Will. "Gay History—April 17, 1965." Back2Stonewall. April 17, 2019. www.back2stonewall.com/2018/04/april-17-1965-gay-history-whitehouseprotest.html.

Lopez, German. "Trump's Ban on Transgender Troops, Explained." Vox. January 22, 2019. www.vox.com/identities/2017/7/26/16034366/trump-transgender-military-ban.

Peters, Jeremy W. "The Decline and Fall of the 'H' Word." *New York Times*, March 21, 2014. www.nytimes.com/2014/03/23/fashion/gays-lesbians-the-term-homosexual.html.

Roschke, Ryan. "Sashay Through the History of Drag Queen Culture." POPSUGAR. September 5, 2019. www.popsugar.com/news/History-Drag-Drag-Queen-Culture-44512387.

Rumore, Kori. "Guide to Chicago's Pride Parade." *Chicago Tribune*, June 26, 2019. www.chicagotribune.com/data/ct-chicago-gay-pride-fest-parade-history-2018-htmlstory.html.

"Terminology for Discussing Gender." Ann & Robert H. Lurie Children's Hospital of Chicago. www.luriechildrens.org/en/specialties-conditions/gender-development-program/resources/terminology-for-discussing-gender/.

Thrasher, Steven. "Bayard Rustin." BuzzFeed. August 27, 2013. www.buzzfeed.com/steventhrasher/walter-naegle-partner-of-the-late-bayard-rustin-talks-about?utm_term=.ku4N2XwdQ#.dtV8Qpd46.

"A Timeline of HIV and AIDS." HIV.gov. www.hiv.gov/hiv-basics/overview/history/hiv-and-aids-timeline.

"Trans History, Linked." Digital Transgender Archive. www.digitaltransgenderarchive.net/.

"Why We March." Reclaim Pride Coalition. reclaimpridenyc.org/why-we-march.

Archival Sources

Making Gay History Podcast
Out History
Lesbian Herstory Archives
ONE Archives
GLBT Historical Society Archive
NYC LGBT Historic Sites Project
The Center
Human Rights Campaign